BARE BONES STONES

A Welcome Guide to Curling

Joel Ingersoll

Cover designed by Bill Jordan Design
http://www.billjordandesign.com

Additional artwork by Duncan York

Joel Ingersoll
Find me on Twitter @FlyoverJoel

Printed in the United States of America

First Printing: Feb 2017

ISBN 978-1-9770275-0-4

For Fiona, a great spouse and an even better lead.

CONTENTS

INTRODUCTION

The best part of the Winter Olympics is how we become experts on every sport within five minutes of cracking open a beer and turning on the TV. It doesn't matter which event we're watching. Our knowledge is encyclopedic and insightful. For those two weeks, we're locked in with a laser-like focus on all the minutiae of sports even though we have no real idea what's going on. Regardless, we're happy to share our expertise with anyone who will listen, which is typically our cats. "They messed up the twizzle! It's the most important ice dance of their careers and they screwed something up that easy! How does that even happen, Monster?" (Our cat, for these purposes, is named Monster and he never has an answer for us). Never mind that the hour before or after our moment of bluster, we couldn't point out a twizzle in a YouTube skating video entitled, "Chock Full o' Twizzles." By the sixth hour of non-stop Olympic level couch sitting, we wipe the puffy cheese ball dust off our face, set down a slice of pizza and gravely say, "I understand that Estonia has a pretty strong biathlon team this year. They can get their post-skiing heart rates down to one beat per minute like those monks everyone thinks are dead," without knowing if Estonia has a biathlon team or if biathletes even compete as a team. After the sixth beer, we can share our historical genius with facts such as, "It's called half pipe because that's the amount they can smoke and still test under the IOC's THC levels." In other words, we are all gems, and our spouses are very lucky to have us.

From the first time someone in Finland said, "Hey Mikko! Hold my beer, I've got my skis and rifle and want to try something!" to that new mogul skiing event called "So You Think You Can Tear Your ACL," Americans have long observed that the Winter Olympic sports are weird. "Here, let's push this giant soap box derby car for a few feet, hop in and ride it down a giant ice slide at a billion miles an hour. You can get former NFL players to push it? Even better." Never mind that the

Summer Olympics have water polo, handball, and dressage (a/k/a fancy horse dancing), it's the Winter Olympic sports that are generally thought of as weird.

No sport is weirder to the American viewing audience than curling, but on the other hand, no team sport generates more curiosity. From its modern debut at the 1998 Nagano Olympics to a dedicated cable channel at Sochi in 2014, curling has become one of the most popular and most talked about Winter Olympic sports. On the first Monday during the Winter Olympics in Sochi, more than five million Americans tuned in to watch curling. That number is particularly impressive when you realize the United States Curling Association didn't hit 20,000 members until 2016. A new viewer's interest generally starts with, "My wife wants me to sweep the kitchen, so I bet I'm really good at curling. Har. Har. Har," and ends with, "you know, I might want to give curling a try." This reaction is likely due to the fact that curling is both accessible to regular folks but challenging enough to stretch the most skilled players. For someone just being introduced to curling, it's also as confusing as hell.

My First Time Curling

The first time I walked into the historic Saint Paul Curling Club in Minnesota, I wasn't sure where to go. I had been nagging a friend for several years about teaching me to curl and he had just signed me up for a league. As I passed the front desk, my friend was already coming my way with a pitcher of beer and poured me a glass. I sat down across from him on a leather couch next to a fireplace, and thought to myself, "These are my people." Although I was happy to be welcomed, I was also worried about slipping on the ice and falling on my head. Despite being an expert on curling from watching it non-stop during the Olympics, I had no idea what I was doing.

Seven years (and a lot of beers) later I've thought a lot about what I would have liked to have known that first time I stepped on the ice. Not a training guide, but more of a roadmap to help explain what and why people were doing what they were doing. I read a "how to" book before curling my first match, but it didn't really help. What I wanted was something to make the game a little more accessible to someone whose only experience was watching curling during the Olympics. Ultimately, most folks learn about curling from trial and error, but a little secondary material would have helped too.

As I progressed from asking "the slider goes where? On my foot? Really?" to wondering why someone threw a guard with the sixth rock in the seventh end instead of a takeout, I noticed that there's a gap in the curling literature. There's no resource falling between an introductory "There Are Four People on Each Team and They Each Throw Two Rocks" and "How to Curl Like a Champion: The Strategy Guide for People Who Emerged from the Womb with a Broom."

Before you settle in to read this book, I'm going to suggest you pour yourself a glass of whiskey or, if you are not of age, apple cider. Roughly halfway through the book, refill your glass. This book is going to be a conversation. When a curling match is complete, the eight players sit around a table, share a drink, and talk about the game. Much like I did after each game that first year, and every year since. I'm fortunate living in Minnesota because I have curling resources that aren't available elsewhere in the United States. The Twin Cities have added over a thousand new curlers in the last seven years, so most of the table conversation revolves around the game in general and not necessarily the game that we've just played. More the "Big G" than the "little g," if you will. That's what this book is about. The things we talk about at the table.

THE ROARING GAME

When the trees start to green and it warms up too much maintain the ice at the Frogtown Curling Club in Saint Paul, Minnesota, I move to the Four Seasons Curling Club out in the suburbs. It's called the Four Seasons not because it's a fancy resort, but because I can curl there in the spring and summer. Four Seasons is close to my office, but in the opposite direction from my home, so I often find myself in their bar, Sticks and Stones, with several hours to kill before my evening league game. This gives me a great opportunity to listen to the hockey moms and dads chatter about their day while slamming a quick chardonnay or beer between periods of watching their small children slowly knock each other over playing at the hockey arena connected to the club. But more fun than watching The Real Hockey Parents of the Twin Cities, is listening locals check out a group curling on the ice.

One afternoon, I plopped down at a table with a pint of beer (known as aiming fluid in the parlance of curling) where two couples were watching a group throw rocks on the ice. "I think the goal is to keep the rock on that centerline for as long as possible," one of the men mused. If you are just hanging out with a plate of nachos and have several matches going on live in front of you, there's no real way to figure out what the players are doing. With that in mind, I joined those two couples and we talked about curling for a few minutes over a beer to fill them in on the bare minimum details of curling.

Curling is nicknamed the "Roaring Game" and is often compared to bocce ball, shuffleboard, or chess on ice. I prefer "Bowling with an Elevated Risk of Concussion," as it's played on ice that is both slippery and hard. The ice surface where curling is played is called a sheet. The bullseye at each end of the sheet is called the house. The thick line beyond each house is called the hog line. The things that look like starters' blocks in racing that the players deliver from are called the hack. Curling ice doesn't have a smooth surface like that used for hockey or figure skating. It's covered in tiny frozen water droplets called pebble. The grinding sound of the rock traveling over the pebble gives the game its nickname.

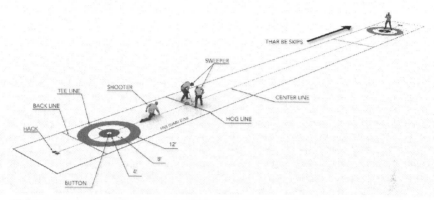

This is what a curling sheet would look like if you could fly like a drone.

Curling is a game played between two teams of four players each (or maybe three if it snows or rush hour is bad before a six o'clock league draw). The four players on a team are the lead, second, third (vice-skip) and skip. Each player on the team throws two consecutive granite rocks with colored plastic handles, alternating between the teams. For example, if the rock handles are red and yellow, and red throws first, the red lead throws, then the yellow lead, then the red lead, then the yellow lead, then the red second, then the yellow second, and so on until all sixteen rocks are thrown. The opposite is true if yellow throws first. The skips typically throw the last four rocks (two each). The sixteenth and final rock is called the hammer. This throwing of sixteen stones is called an end, which is similar to an inning in baseball. In recreational curling, games have eight ends or fewer, while in competitive curling, teams play ten ends.

The goal in throwing those rocks from one end of the sheet to the other end is to have the most rocks closest to the center of the house after all sixteen rocks have been delivered. Points are awarded only after everyone has thrown all their rocks, i.e., at the end of an end (confused yet?). Only one team can score in each end. The team that scores is the one with the stone closest to the center of the house. If the team with the closest rock to the center also has the second closest rock to the button, they get two points. That team continues to score points until an opponent's rock is closer which stops this counting process.

It's important to remember that scoring doesn't start until all the rocks are thrown. Curlers don't just throw each rock to the button repeatedly and hope for the

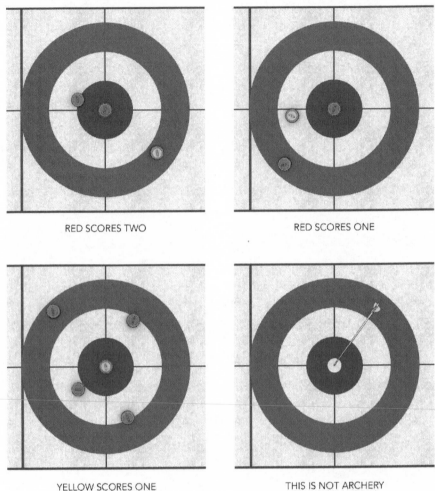

RED SCORES TWO

RED SCORES ONE

YELLOW SCORES ONE

THIS IS NOT ARCHERY

best. Instead, players throw guards, draws, and hits in varying permutations in the hopes of having rocks in scoring position after all the rocks are thrown. To throw a stone, a curler places one foot upon a small slanted foothold called the hack and the other foot on the ice. He or she pushes off from the hack, slides down the ice, and releases the rock with clockwise or counterclockwise rotation prior to reaching the hog line.

Once a player delivers the rock toward the other end of the sheet, two of the shooter's teammates sweep in front of the stone with a broom that has a synthetic pad on the end. This sweeping temporarily melts the pebble in front of the rock, reducing friction. Reducing the friction causes the stone to curl less, travel farther and hopefully land in the appropriate location. Sweeping cannot cause the rock to suddenly stop or go in the opposite direction of the stone's rotation. The player who isn't sweeping or throwing stands in the house opposite to the player throwing. This person uses their broom to provide a target for the shot and yells instructions to the sweepers as the rock travels down the ice to adjust for the curl of the stone and how far it is expected to travel. Once the game has concluded, teams shake hands and meet in the club room for a beer or two and proceed to lie about the amazing shots they took during the game.

Congratulations! You now know the barest minimum to watch and understand curling. I hope it wasn't too painful. The rest of the book provides more detail and background information about curling so that you too can start to expound on curling strategy like a true expert. Just remember to wipe the cheese ball dust off your face first.

A BRIEF HISTORY OF CURLING

N ot to brag or anything, but I've read John Kerr's 1890 tome *History of Curling*. You should be happy I did this; it means you don't have to read paragraphs like this one:

The volume having greatly exceeded the limits originally designed, it has been found necessary to omit a Glossary of Curling Words and Phrases, also a large collection of Songs and Humorous Stories marked as worthy of preservation. The ground having been so far cleared by this "History," justice may yet be done to the other subjects referred to, in a second volume, which will be forthcoming whenever an earnest demand is made for its production. The trouble and anxiety connected with the preparation and publication of a work such as this commemorative volume is have been great; but these, it is believed, will soon be forgotten if by its means a fresh enthusiasm be inspired in a game which develops all that is manly and good in social life, and unites in one brotherhood all ranks and conditions of men.

I'm pretty sure Mr. Kerr exceeded the limits originally designed for the piece in just this discussion about the original limits. I bet his blog would be a real hoot. As far as I can tell, there never was a volume two of the *History of Curling* since it's now 2017 and we aren't celebrating Kerr as the oldest living person on the planet. Perhaps the demand was there but wasn't earnest enough.

Verbosity aside, Kerr's volume is extremely thorough and carefully takes the reader through major curling milestones that happened, from the first historical references of curling all the way up to the fiftieth anniversary of the Royal Caledonian Curling club in 1888 and his writing of a book on the history of curling. I'm not prone to hyperbole, but I'm pretty sure his last sentence was, "and then I added a period to this sentence and the book was finished." I'm not going to be that rigorous here, but I still want to give you a brief overview of the origins and history of curling.

Like many sports, curling started with a couple of dudes making up a game to pass the time, which then evolved into a sport managed by a cohesive international governing body (largely defined by revising rules for the sport and collecting dues). In the case of curling, a windswept game of Calvinball on the frozen lochs of Scotland transformed into the game we watch today where curlers scream loudly on our high-def televisions. Kerr describes the origins of curling as "lost to mists of antiquity" which is really a fancy way of saying "we don't know."

After setting the stage with a discussion of ancient Egyptians and infants nursing on goats (he's that thorough), Kerr gets down to business. He explains that certain words and concepts associated with curling seem to be of Scottish origin, while a handful of others are of Germanic origin. For most people, this might be problematic, but for Kerr, it's cool because he is convinced curling was invented in Scotland. His general thesis is that, just like golf, curling is a Scottish game and all those wannabes from the continent can suck it, like those babies with the goats. Also, golf is all right and all, but curling is much cooler. I feel the same way, Mr. Kerr, no matter how conflicted I am about your baby goat suckers.

The oldest known curling stone dates from 1511. Since there isn't much in the way of funding for carbon dating curling stones, we are rather fortunate the date was etched into it. This stone has more of a knob than a handle. Earlier curling stones simply had spots to place a thumb and forefinger, kind of like a bowling ball. Most of these bygone stones are found tucked away in barns, under stairs, or in pond bottoms because it turns out that curling stones aren't exactly buoyant. Unlike pots and pans, where rapid fingerprint loss makes handles a rather obvious design improvement, it took a little while for our intrepid Scots to add them to their curling stones. Early curling stones weren't particularly uniform in size or shape. Instead, they were collected by players who thought "Hey, this might make a good stone for curling." As late as the 1830s, some folks were still bragging about their seventy-pound stones. Today, if a curler says they have seventy-pound stones, it means something completely different and they may have difficulty walking. During the earlier era, curling was also BYOR, and those who had rocks more suited to the game were more successful. Much like the Broomgate controversy we will discuss later in the book, the emergence of advanced rock technology led to the standardization of curling rocks we see today.

Outside of dated curling stones, we have several other artifacts which highlight the early days of curling. In print, there is a 1541 reference from Scottish notary John McQuhin who recorded a stone throwing challenge between John Sclater, a monk at Paisley Abbey and another gentleman with the name of Gavin Hamilton. This may be the first written reference to curling unless something even earlier pops up. I know it weirds me out every time I see my online fantasy football results from a decade ago; I can't imagine having my descendants see the results of my curling match from centuries ago.

Two other early references to curling appear in paintings. The Library of Canada website has two paintings by Pietr Bruegel dating from approximately 1565. The first, *Winter Landscape with a Bird Trap* shows people curling on a river with a bird trap in the foreground, hence its name. The second, *Hunters in the Snow* shows a pair of hunters in the foreground with a pack of dogs, overlooking several dozen curlers on the ice who will presumably be their dinner.

No mention of curling history would be complete without referencing the great Scottish poet Robert Burns. Seriously, all of the citizens Scotland would burn their books in protest. As Bob Cowen, the former editor of *Scottish Curler* magazine explains in The Curling History Blog, "Yes, Burns WAS a curler, despite what it might say in older books, and some respected websites that have not been updated." I'm not going to argue with the all caps usage of "was," and just say the Burns poem *Tam Samson's Elegy* clearly talks about curling.

Early curling matches in Scotland were played between parishes. The matches slowly became more organized, which ultimately led to the formation of the Caledonian Curling Club in Edinburgh on July 25, 1838. In 1842, Queen Victoria was treated to a curling demonstration in the ballroom of Scone Palace, where it was probably somewhat warmer but less icy, which ultimately lead to the granting of a royal designation to the club in 1843. The newly minted Royal Caledonian Curling Club codified the rules of the game and functioned as an international governing body in the early days of curling. In 1907, the first indoor rink was built in Scotland, which started the progression of curling to the version of the game we play today.

As Scots migrated from their homelands to Canada and the United States, they brought curling with them. Their small curling clubs dotted the landscape. Every small-town Canadian I know has a few stories about these community clubs being an important aspect of social life in their towns. Unfortunately, these clubs are falling by the wayside. It doesn't seem to be lack of interest that's the problem, but expense. Curling is rather expensive to play because a club's maintenance costs are high. Throwing a cup of water in the freezer is cheap but making ice in a barn big enough for four sheets of ice isn't. While economies of scale can help ease those costs, the risks are also high. Opening a big club during the Olympics when demand is high might sound like a great idea, but if it doesn't catch on you'll have exponentially higher costs than if you stayed with a small venue and just skated by on league fees, club dues, a bar (if you're lucky) and any groups you can book during the day and on weekends. This isn't to hijack the section on the history of curling to discuss the financial problems of many curling clubs, but instead to highlight the challenges which will eventually become part of curling's past.

The Tim Horton's Brier is the world's foremost men's curling tournament in the world. It is held in rotating locations around Canada and features the best teams in the country. So, it's not like curling just pops out of the attic every four years, stretches and asks what it missed. The Brier dates back to 1925 and was designed as an event to bring the east and west of Canada together through curling. The current sponsor, Tim Horton's is Canada's beloved version of Dunkin' Donuts, even though the real Tim Horton was a hockey player, not a curler. While he passed away in 1974, the best equivalent I can come up with is if Minnesota Viking and NFL MVP Alan Page started a coffee and donut shop with six franchises in every city in the United States. That is Tim Horton's. Tim Horton's has been the sponsor of the Brier since 2006 and is heavily involved in a number of major events as a sponsor. In fact, at many events on the tour, they even put out coffee and Timbits for the players because nothing says competitive curling like getting jacked up on caffeine and sugar before a big game (If you are not familiar with Timbits, they are magical Canadian donut holes. This is what my Canadian wife led me to believe during our two hours wait for some when a Tim Horton's opened at the Mall of America). While Tim Horton's is synonymous with the Brier today, this wasn't always the case. Every province, territory, Northern Ontario and the designated Team Canada has a chance to play in the Tim Horton's Brier.

Just like everywhere else, women curlers were excluded from having fun for far too long because the patriarchy is absolutely terrible. It wasn't until 1960 that the Canadian Ladies' Curling Association was formed. By 1961, they were already holding a national tournament in the mold of the Brier because if it takes men three hundred years to organize an event, it'll take women about one. The first Scott Tournament of Hearts, a true sister to the Brier, debuted in 1982. Over one hundred thousand people attended the 2017 Brier in St. John's, Newfoundland and another fifty-six thousand made their way to watch the Scotties in St. Catharines, Ontario. In 2015, over 7.5 million unique Canadians watched the Brier on television and that same year and the Scotties averaged 579,000 viewers per televised game. Together, the Brier and Scotties are the two most recognizable and watched annual curling events in the world.

Despite the late start in competitive curling compared to the men, the women worked really hard to catch up in one November weekend in 2017. Summerside, Prince Edward Island, hosted the Road to the Roar, an event which offered teams the opportunity to play into the Roar of the Rings, Canada's festively named Olympic qualifying tournament. After round robin play, five of the seven women's teams in Pool A were tied with a 3-3 record, but there were only two available playoff spots. One team qualified for the playoffs for being better than 3-3, while the five 3-3 teams had to play tie-breaking games to advance to the playoffs. The last draw wrapped up around 2:45 am on Friday night and the team that survived all the tiebreakers was then rewarded with even more curling. Life lesson: What's the reward for doing a good job at work? More work.

For a Road to the Roar team to make the Olympics, they would need to advance from a field of fourteen teams and then knock out an additional eight teams at the Roar of the Rings. I love curling but, no joke, that's a lot of curling. While the tiebreakers weren't as dramatic on the men's side, any team in Canada has to travel this road to advance to the Olympics. In contrast, the United States only required Team Nina Roth to win in a pool of three teams and Team John Shuster win in a group of five. This was a much quicker path to the Olympics than Canada's "falling asleep while watching curling because it's way past my bedtime" extravaganza.

Curling was a demonstration sport at the inaugural Olympic Winter Games in 1924. At least that is what everyone thought until 2006, when the IOC said, "Nope, it was completely legitimate. We overlooked telling you guys for the last eighty-two years." Curling made a demonstration appearance again in 1932 and then took a long nap until reappearing in the 1988 and 1992 games. Curling officially became a Winter Olympic sport for the second time at Nagano, Japan, in 1998. The Winter Paralympic

Games included wheelchair curling in 2006 after the first world championships were held in 2002.

The 2018 Winter Games will feature Mixed Doubles curling for the first time, which if you think that regular old curling is weird, mixed doubles is twice as weird with just half the number of players. This is not to give the short shrift to Wheelchair Curling or Mixed Doubles; we'll discuss more of the relative newcomers to the curling scene after we've set a baseline for regular old curling for comparison.

THE SHEET

When walking out onto a curling sheet from the back, you'll need to step over a back bumper to get on the ice. These are portable foam bars designed to protect the back of the sheet from any rocks that go sailing through the house and are not caught, and from general bumps from pushing rocks out of the play area. If you are watching competitive events, you may notice bumpers change every couple of ends to feature a different advertiser. Bumpers are not always affixed to the end of the sheet, but instead may be free-floating, which is also what you will be if you accidentally step on one. As you proceed down the sheet, the next landmark is the hack, A right-handed curler throws out of the left hack and a left-handed curler out of the right hack. Rules prohibit throwing from the opposite hack and you really don't want to try and throw with one foot in each if you enjoy the current shape of your nose. Past the hack will be the back line. As the name suggests, it is the line marking the back of the playing surface, which meets the back of the house. A rock needs to completely cross the back line to be considered out of play. In my experience, throwing a rock through the back of the house on accident is disturbingly easy.

We have now reached the house, which is the giant bullseye on each end of the sheet. The outermost circle is called the twelve-foot as it is twelve feet in diameter. The next circle in is usually white and is called the eight-foot, as it is, you guessed it, eight feet in diameter. The next circle is the four-foot. Finally, you have a full white circle, rather than a ring, and that's called the button. There's a tiny hole in the center of the button called the pin. A measuring device (that's its real name, it might as well be called a measuring thingie) gets placed in the pin if players need to determine which rock is scoring or whether a rock is in the house. To be in the house and in scoring position, only the smallest portion of the rock needs to be over top of the twelve-foot ring. We say over the top because the running band on the bottom of the stone is significantly smaller than the circumference of the rock. In essence, a scoring rock's butt can be outside the house, but its belly overtop the twelve.

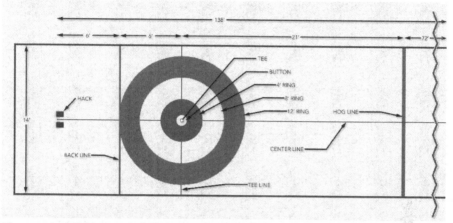

There are lots of things on a curling sheet, fortunately only a few can be tripped over.

In the center of the house, there are two straight lines. One goes the length of the sheet to the other house and is called the centerline. The other runs perpendicular to the centerline in the middle of the house and is called the tee line because it intersects with the centerline to form a "t" at the pin. As a point of reference, we will talk about the tee line quite a bit. In terms of gameplay, only one player can sweep their own rocks behind the tee line. A skip can sweep an opponent's rock once it crosses the tee line to try and carry it out of play.

Walking up the sheet twenty-one feet from the tee line, the next landmark you reach is the hog line. The hog line, like nearly everything else in Scotland, refers to sheep. It's a thick line that runs on each end of the sheet past the house. A shooter must release the rock prior to reaching the near hog line (the hog line on the shooting end) or it's a violation and the rock is taken out of play. Once the stone is delivered, it must cross the far hog line (the hog line the closest to the house to which you are shooting) to stay in play. If a rock comes up short and fails to completely cross that line, it is considered hogged and taken out of play. The only exception to this is if the shooter's rock strikes another rock in play, so is unable to cross the far hog line. In seven years, I've seen this happen twice and it was adventurously accomplished on back-to-back shots.

You might be wondering at this point, "Boy this all sounds very interesting, but what do hogs have to do with curling?" Well, it turns out that a hog is a term for a young sheep who is likely to trail behind the flock, fall ill, or be culled. The runt of the litter. A rock that isn't powerful enough to cross the other hog-line is considered hogged and is culled from play. A sport that prides itself on cheering an opponent's great shot also compares the dreadful experience of severely underthrowing a rock to a dead baby sheep—which seems rather unsporting.

At this point, you will stop moving forward to the other end of the sheet. It's not because there isn't anything interesting down there, but rather that the far end of the sheet is a mirror image of what you've just looked at. Turning left or right takes us to the sidelines which are the final part of a curling sheet. Unlike the back line, if even a hair of the rock is over a sideline, it is taken out of play. The reason for this is most curling clubs do not have any kind of physical barrier between separate sheets, so any rock crossing the sideline ends up on the next sheet's field of play. Only in championship events where an arena is specially converted for curling do you have luxuriously carpeted walkways between every sheet. Most curling clubs are only as big as they need to be to accommodate four, six or even eight sheets with just a few walkways among the sheets if you are lucky. Those walkways are very valuable for ice makers. It's a lot easier to flood and manage three groups of two sheets than it is to flood and level six sheets. That's all predicated on whether the building was built specifically for curling and whether curlers were involved, rather than other ice sports people, in the design. Most clubs don't have the luxury of having full-blown separators between the sheets, and sweepers really need to be conscious about catching rocks that are going out of play and potentially crossing the sidelines into an adjacent game.

PLAYERS

Here's what they don't tell you in all the curling primers: the skip and vice-skip are independent of the throwing position. If you had a peek at the pregame paperwork for a competitive event, there is a place on the lineup card to identify who will be throwing lead, second, third, fourth, and then there's a separate space to designate a skip and vice-skip. When explaining curling to the uninitiated, it's easier to say that the vice-skip throws third in the rotation and the skip throws fourth. However, any player on the team can be the skip or vice-skip regardless of which rocks they throw. I regularly curl with a guy who is a better shooter than I am, so he throws fourth, but I still skip because I have control issues that I might want to talk with someone about. This configuration is atypical, so we will focus on the traditional line-up. The lead throws the first two rocks of the end and then sweeps the next six rocks. The second throws the next two rocks, numbers three and four. The vice-skip throws the fifth and six rocks and then holds the broom and calls line for the skip. The skip throws the last two rocks of the end and calls the first six shots. The lead and second on a team are the "front end," and the vice and skip are the "back end." For a curling team, figuring out where each player goes in a horse costume at Halloween is easy.

The skip is the captain of the team and the team name derives from the skip's last name. If Nina Roth is skipping the team, then the team will be named Team Roth or could be called the Roth Rink. This is also true of beer leagues and fun bonspiels except for those teams who love puns. In bonspiels or league play, you might see teams called Broom Goes the Dynamite, On the Rocks, No Sweep 'til Brooklyn, and these people are terrible (just kidding, you guys). In the Olympics, teams are designated by their country.

Lead

The lead is an enigma, wrapped in a conundrum, explained by this terrible metaphor. In club play, leads are almost always the least experienced player on the team. If you add someone new, you slot them into the lead spot. Have a curler who is less interested in improving than the others? Pencil them in here. Seems logical: in each end you have six rocks to recover from whatever mayhem a less skilled player may have created by throwing the first two rocks. On the other hand, in competitive play, the lead may be the most important position on a team after the skip. This is true for two reasons. First, leads set up each end of the game. Strong guards, draws and hits from the lead position mean teams are playing with an advantage, not playing from behind in the end and chasing the opponent. Steve Buttery (@ch4ndsd) posted a quick analysis to Twitter of the importance of each position in relation to shooting percentage and the team's won/loss record. His analysis proposed that the skip shooting well was the primary factor when a team wins. This makes sense. The next most important factor predicting victory was the lead's shooting percentage. Leads are expected to make 99% of their shots, whether it be a guard, draw, hit or wick (these types of shots are all explained in depth later in the book, I promise), yet they are often throwing without any other rocks on the sheet, challenging the shooter's perspective. On the other hand, skips may be throwing more difficult shots but are more likely to be in the 85%-90% range if they are shooting really well. A strong shooting lead dictates how the end plays out and makes a skip's job easier.

The second reason why leads are important is that they watch six consecutive rocks each end. They throw their two and then sweep the rest. Out of anyone on the team, they should have the best sense of how fast the ice is running and where there may be unusual spots that may slow down a stone or keep a stone carrying. This is valuable information as the ice continues to change over the course of a game. My wife and I have shuffled positions over the years, but our teams really made a huge jump when she moved to lead. Having her to set up an end with guards and freezes, track the behavior of the ice, and then effectively communicate that information to the team is a huge advantage in our beer, wine, and crockpot leagues.

Second

The second sweeps the first two stones of the end. They then throw the third and fourth rocks for the team and then sweep the final four. While all curlers need to be able to throw all types of shots, if the end is properly set up by the lead, the second may have to throw a takeout with their first shot and then turn around and make a draw with the next. Seconds need to be flexible. It's hard to dial down the adrenaline of that first hit, so seconds must be versatile enough to throw different kinds of shots back-to-back without being influenced by the previous shot. For example, throwing a peel (a very heavy takeout) on the first shot is hard enough, but then coming back forty-five seconds later to throw a draw to the top of the lid (the button, or center of the house), or a come-around freeze (a rock that curls around a guard and touches a stationary stone) that may end up as the scoring rock for the end is exceptionally hard.

Sweeping is hard work. World-class curlers on television make it look easy. They gracefully slide down the ice for a hundred feet while brushing furiously, and then glide back to do it again a minute later. For those of us who aren't in Olympic condition, it is an exhausting endeavor. It also makes shooting that much more difficult. Getting into the hack and tossing a soft draw isn't easy when you are breathing heavily and have an elevated heart rate from vigorously sweeping (we can't all be Estonian biathletes, after all). This is a skill needed by both seconds and thirds as they are the two players who have to go immediately from sweeping to shooting. It is even more challenging when your glasses fog up from the cold and you can't see anything in front of you. Seconds are also critical to understanding the ice. Between the lead and second, one player will time all of the rocks thrown in an end to get a determination of weight while the other will measure the rock on instinct. Communication between the lead and second is important for making sure the rock ends up in the location called by the skip.

Third/Vice-Skip

Vice-skips sweep the lead's and second's rocks and then hold the broom and call the line for the skip's shots. They are the only player on the team who gets exposure to both weight (the distance the rock will travel) from sweeping, and to line (how much the rock will curl) from calling the skip's shots throughout the game. All this back and forth means the vice-skips have the hardest position on the team. They have to be able to manage both the front and back end. They are the primary communicator between the skip and front end because they sweep half of the rocks each end. On the back end, they are calling the line for the skip's rocks, which will likely determine the outcome of the end. Vice-skips may also be a team's best all-around shooter as they may need to clean up (hit several rocks out of play) after the front end or throw softer shots to set up a scoring chance for the skip. Vice-skips must also do math, which is terrible, as they oversee working with the opponent's vice-skip to determine the score for each end. In league play, they also have the task of managing the coin flip for hammer before the game. If the NFL has taught us anything about coin flipping, it's not that easy.

Skip

I skip two teams, but the first question I get asked by non-curling people is, "are you one of the sweepers?" If you asked my teammates, the answer is no. Generally, I say, "I'm the yeller." They nod sagely, because in some strange way that makes total sense. I'm the loud guy who yells. Skips do sweep, however, just not very often, but when they do their teammates want to make sure they are on it. I've had times where I'm more than adequately sweeping a rock out of the back of the house and my teammates, former teammates, and random friends on other sheets will be screaming "HARD! HARD! HARD!" at me between giggles because I've done something to deserve that treatment in my life. Sometimes, skips will make a show of being the third sweeper on a light rock, although the efficacy of the third sweeper is debatable. As curler and sweeping expert Dean Gemmell recently told a young skip at a clinic, "You look ridiculous. Science has proven the third sweeper has no effect, so their job is to stay in the house and yell." Skips can also sweep their opponent's rocks once they've crossed the tee line and are heading to the back of the house. In club play, they may also sweep a rock the entire way down the ice after an early end bathroom break. All this is to say that a skip isn't just expending mental energy and yelling at everyone; we occasionally sweep.

Maybe we shouldn't be so hard on skips and their sweeping, or lack thereof. Skips are under a lot of pressure during a game. First and foremost, skips are the game manager. Skips call each shot during the end in an attempt to make sure they have the opportunity to score points when their final shots come around. They are expected to know and understand how each player shoots on their team, what their strengths and weaknesses are, and how to maximize those under changing ice conditions. If the vice-skip is better at draws than hits, skips may tailor the shot selection to get more freezes and guards from the vice-skip, with the intent on hitting them later in the end to score multiple points. If they are playing a team that draws well, then the skip will be more focused on hitting out guards rather than drawing around them. It's a massive amount of information to process for each shot, and skips need to do it quickly, so they don't run out of time in a game.

Skips also have to make the most pressure-filled shots each end. To be fair, they are also the ones whose shots are often memorialized in videos that make me yell, "Holy Crap! Babe! Come in here! You have to see this shot!" every five minutes, ensuring my wife gets her 10,000 steps in for the day. Skips need to be able to draw to the button to score, or, maybe, more importantly, save a team from giving up a bad end.

I played in a charity event with Canada's amazing Val Sweeting against the United States' John Shuster. I was vice-skipping and seemed pretty comfortable with our two rocks sitting near the button and then not so comfortable when I watched Shuster slam his rock on the inside of a stone in the outside twelve-foot and roll it right on the button for a point. This is not to suggest I've tried the same shots since seeing that great hit, but skips need to be open to the entire realm of possibilities on each shot, and they also have to make them.

A Bit More on Players

Quite a number of people watched the movie *Cool Runnings* and thought to themselves, "By God! If the Jamaicans can bobsled, so can I!" and that dream of being an Olympian lasted a few months before being supplanted with another one to get them through the workday. The same is true of curling. Facebook is awash in pictures of people splayed out on the ice with either the caption, "I'm going to be an Olympian!" or a comment on that picture that asks, "Are you going to be an Olympian now? LOL!" and that's a big part of what makes curling fun. In America, we think of curling as an Olympic sport, so the pinnacle of achievement is winning the Olympics. It reminds us of when we were little and dreamed big. Now, I don't want to wither those hopes, but there's some stuff you should know about the curlers who really do make their Olympic dreams come true.

Despite receiving modest cash tips on two separate occasions for providing coaching during corporate learn-to-curl events, I'm not what you'd describe as a professional curler. To be honest though, in the United States there aren't any professional curlers if you define professional as full-time. In fact, even for Canadians, who dominate the sport, players don't earn enough from curling for it to be full-time either. Unless they are independently wealthy, competitive curlers are also physical therapists, restaurant managers, IT professionals, and engineers who work for very understanding companies and bosses. Essentially, they're the same as us, except for the understanding companies and bosses part.

Even with five curling clubs in the Twin Cities, ice time can be difficult to get. It's not unusual to have a national-level player competing in your rec league. This is not every day, and it might not be their entire competitive team, but all of a sudden, there you are curling against someone who competes at an elite level and you are figuring out how to make a game of it. I know I wouldn't want to find myself lined up across from Vernon Davis and have to stop him from catching a football, and/or clinging to his ankle as he drags me down the field leaving a trail of my teeth in his wake during a flag football game. I'm not suggesting the skill level between elite players and average curlers isn't significant, because it is, but rather that there's a level of interaction and intimacy in curling that flavors the dynamic of the sport for all skill levels of players.

Curling is a hard-enough sport to master, and it's even harder when you can't dedicate three hours a day to practicing all year round. In the 2016–2017 World Curling Season, Rachel Homan's team earned $132,500 (in the greatest currency of all, Loonies) on the tour. That sounds great for any sport. But, remember when you divide those winnings by four, you are down to a hair over $33,000 for each player. And before you can even do that, you must eliminate the cost of flights, hotels, and food. Since a lot of these events start on Wednesdays or Thursdays you need to add those additional days to the cost. At least Canadians players have guaranteed health insurance, whereas in the US they don't. Missed time from work also costs players income. After all these costs, $33,000 in prize money doesn't stretch very far at all. Of course, teams like Homan's also have sponsors and other sources of funding, but only a handful of players in the world can make enough money to not have a day job. All of this is to say, is if you are a marketing person working for a large company, these folks could use a few bucks and you could use a patch or logo on their jacket.

SWEEPING

The most frequently asked question about curling is, "what's up with the broom thingies?" As the most identifiable aspect of curling and the most mysterious for the very casual observer, once we've outlined who all the players are, we have to explain sweeping. Because it's cold at my home club, we begin learn-to-curl events with sweeping. Our philosophy is to get people on the ice and teach them to sweep first, so they get the blood flowing and warm up.

Sweeping the stone serves several purposes. First, it removes debris from in front of the path of the stone. Second, curling ice isn't smooth, it's bumpy. Sweeping melts those bumps and reduces the friction between the rock and the ice, allowing it to travel further and straighter than it would on its own. Elite level sweepers can carry a stone a good eight to ten feet further than it might otherwise travel. Finally, sweeping provides a reliable excuse for the shooter when they miss a shot.

Debris on the ice is more of an issue that you might think. One would guess that a forty-two pound stone traveling a hundred feet in fourteen seconds wouldn't be bothered by a little piece of pant lint, but one would be incorrect. Even the tiniest bit of fuzz can catch in the running band of the stone and slow it down significantly, make it hook or fade in one direction, or even stop it dead in its tracks. Curlers are regularly cleaning their broom heads and picking things up off the ice. You may see players sweeping the projected path of a stone before a shot is thrown in an effort to make sure the path is clean. A lot of that is habit over actual need, but it highlights how much impact ice detritus can have on a game. In years past, a skip might be out on the ice with a glass of rye in one hand and a cigar in the other while calling a game. While increased concern for DUIs and lung cancer have probably improved the game, it most definitely has improved the quality of the ice. A player may sweep lightly in front of a rock, called cleaning, to make sure nothing impedes the forward movement of the rock, but on today's ice, you no longer need a kilted Scotsman vigorously brooming snow, giant piles of spilled ash, or a Eurasian Lynx out of the way.

When a player is about to deliver a rock, sweepers are positioned on each side of the shooter. Those players can be as close to the shooter as they want, but they need to be careful they aren't blocking the shooter's view of the other house, or in the way of the sliding shooter. Newer curlers tend to start far away from the shooter at the hog line and move closer to the shooter as they get more experienced. By positioning them close to the shooter, sweepers can gauge how fast the rock will be delivered well before they need to start sweeping. Once the rock is released, players can begin to sweep the rock. The need to sweep is predicated on how hard the stone is thrown and whether it's on target. Some shots will be swept immediately upon their release while others may need little to no sweeping at all.

To sweep the stone, players have the broom on their outside hip (the side away from the stone) with the hand closest to the stone lower on the broom handle. This is known as having an open-faced grip, meaning the player is facing the skip. For safety reasons, this is how new curlers are taught to sweep a rock. The broom on the outside hip ensures the players are walking forward and with the stone. Walking backward reduces the amount of force a sweeper can put on the broom, and significantly increases the risk of falls and injuries. Research from Dr. Thomas Jenkyn at the University of Western Ontario proposes that a closed position may be more effective for sweeping, but that it requires the sweeper to work on footwork and body positioning to be moving forward toward the skip while sweeping. Ultimately, the advantage is to have the dominant hand lower on the broom to generate more force while sweeping. Considering that most of us are righties that means one player sweeps in the open position and the other in the closed position.

Regardless of the position, the player presses their weight on the broom and moves the broom back-and-forth in front of the stone. The broom head only needs to move a few inches in front of the rock as the running band of the rock on the ice is significantly smaller than the full circumference of the stone. The broom should be at a forty-five-degree angle to the ice in order to provide the best leverage to generate both speed and pressure on the ice. Sweeping dramatically and covering a lot of ice may seem impressive, but it isn't effective for making the rock carry further or stay straight. It's just a way to expend energy and justify an extra beer after the match.

In the context of the game, we talked about who can sweep and when in the section about players. Anyone on the shooting team can sweep a delivered rock before it reaches the far tee line, including the shooter and the skip (although there are doubts about the efficacy and Dean Gemmell may yell at them). Players can also sweep all of their own stones that are struck prior to the tee line; similarly, the non-shooting team can sweep any of their own stones that are hit prior to the tee line. Once a rock gets to the tee line, however, things change. After the tee line, only one player on each team can sweep. Skips or vice-skips can decide on which of the many stones in the back of the house they want to sweep. However, there can only be one, like *The Highlander*.

There are other rules that apply to sweeping but the most common infraction is burning the stone. This is when a sweeper hits a moving rock with their broom. If a rock is burned prior to reaching the far hog line, the rock is removed from play. If it happens after the hog line, there are three possible outcomes. The burned rock can be taken out of play and all of the rocks are put back to where they were originally. The stone[s] can be placed where they would have ended up if no infraction occurred. Or the non-shooting team can choose to do nothing about it. The last of the three is the most likely to happen in club play. The impact of clipping a slow-moving stone is rather minimal and it's not worth the potential bad will from making a stink about it, but ultimately, they choose among the three options at the non-shooting skip's discretion.

In competitive curling, such as the Olympics, you may see two sweepers moving down the ice but only one sweeping at a time. This is called directional sweeping and springs from the idea that sweeping one side of the rock can make a slight impact on how the rock curls down the ice. You'll often see just one player sweeping while the other one comes down the ice largely for moral support and for looking handsome while they carry their broom. When a team really needs to carry the rock for distance, you will see both sweeping early and the whole way down. This is the most effective way to get the rock down the ice and ensure that it does not over curl because it's light. Sweeping on the high side (sweeping into the curl) of the rock will cause the rock to curl a hair more than two people sweeping from each side of the rock. Sweeping against the curl will cause it to stay straighter. Teams will start out sweeping on the low side and then when the rock needs to curl, they will switch to help the rock finish at the end. This is really only applicable at the upper echelons of curling where players are missing by fractions of an inch rather than by feet, like me. How much this directional sweeping helps is debatable though, especially when a rock intended to go to the button hits off the side of a guard because only one person was sweeping the rock.

According to my Fitbit, sweepers walk between two and three miles per game. Couple that with vigorous brushing and keeping your balance on the ice and you get a pretty good cardio workout for a two-hour game. Of course, recreational curling is hardly ever a negative calorie sport when you add in the pre-, post-, and in-game refreshments. Despite what an American Airlines gate agent might tell you when you try to carry on your brooms, curling is a sport. It's hard work and I don't know why I feel the need to justify this other than being defensive about "the sport with the broom thingies" being part of curling's zeitgeist.

ICE

Curling ice is bumpy like those Tupperware bowls your mom bought in the Eighties. The sound of the granite stone sliding on top of those bumps is why curling is called the roaring game and not because early Romans who curled in Scotland were fed to lions. Ice makers don't trot out a Zamboni to prepare the ice. If they did, you could throw a stone with all your strength and it might go fifteen feet before the friction of the surface stops it. To combat this friction problem, ice makers use a piece of equipment that looks like a steampunk jetpack to spray water droplets on the ice to make what is called pebble. A metal blade is then pushed over the bumps to even them out in a process called nipping. The curling stone traveling over the pebble provides significantly less total contact between the rock and the ice. The remaining friction of the stone on the ice combines with the rotation of the stone to cause the rock to curl. As the rock slows down, the stone's curl becomes much more pronounced. When players sweep the ice, the pebble melts a little bit and through a sexy-sounding process called wet friction, and the rock glides on that surface. Sweeping makes the rock travel farther and straighter.

There's not one way to pebble the ice, and ice makers are always experimenting. Some pebble sizes and distribution can create ice that curls a lot (called swingy ice) or just a little (straight ice). The overarching goal of ice making is consistency--from sheet to sheet and from game to game. There will always be environmental factors that cause deviations from consistent ice. Sheets that are next to walls tend to be frostier. The same thing can happen if part of the club has a lower ceiling than the rest. Ice may be different because some sheets had groups use them during the day while others were unused. All of this affects the ice and the ice maker attempts, to the best of their ability, to mitigate these problems so the rocks are consistent, and players learn to trust the ice they are playing on. The best ice makers make consistent ice. They also have very thick skins as it's easy for players to blame missed shots on the ice rather than on lack of skill. In order of magnitude, players blame the ice, then the sweepers, and then the line call, or all three, but unsurprisingly, not themselves.

Not only does curling eschew the Zamboni, but curling ice is typically warmer than hockey ice. At the Four Seasons Curling Club, curlers share ice equipment with the hockey facilities in the same building but don't have any kind of bypass in the system to have different ice temperatures for the two surfaces. Even one degree can make a huge difference. Turning up the ice temperature to twenty-five degrees may make fantastic curling ice, but that may not be cold enough to quickly freeze a layer of water dropped by a Zamboni between periods of a hockey game. Imagine having a thermostat battle with your wife, but instead of just one wife, you are married to the entire Thursday night women's rec hockey league. That's the challenge they have at Four Seasons.

I've been minimally involved with the ice making process. I volunteered once to get up at 2:30 in the morning to help flood our facility before going to work. Making ice is like watching paint dry or grass grow, but colder and wetter.

Here's the basic process for making curling ice. Turn on the ice freezing equipment. With a hose, walk around the facility filling it with about an inch of water. Wait for it to freeze. If you flood again before the previous flood has frozen, the lower layers of ice will crack, and you'll have veins streaking all over the sheet. Do this for two days straight and you have the base layer of ice. Now it's time to shave the ice. It seems counter-intuitive to shave the ice you are trying to create, but ice doesn't magically freeze flat and level. Shaving evens out those peaks and valleys. After shaving, flood several more times. Then paint the ice white. If you don't paint the ice, the color of the pipes and other materials below the ice show through, and it can appear like you decided to make pee ice instead of normal ice. All this time, a team of people is moving the hoses around to keep them from sitting still on the ice because the water in the hoses is above freezing and the hoses can melt the ice. After the white paint dries, a pass is made again with water to seal the paint. After that coat of ice is complete, it's time to put down the rings, lines and any designs on the ice. Some clubs will paint these, while others will put down prefabricated designs. Guess what's next? Flood the ice again to seal the lines and rings. The general rule of ice making is, "Never. Stop. Flooding." When the ice is ready, it's time to put the rocks on the ice and play some games. However, make sure you've cooled the rocks prior to putting them on the ice. The last thing you want on your pristine curling ice is moderately warm granite.

There are four types of curling ice: championship (or slam), dedicated, arena and outdoor. If you picked up this book because you are watching the Winter Olympics, the teams are playing on championship ice. Typically, this will be an arena where the ice is meticulously prepared with laser levels. Water that's treated to a specific pH is used. Things like airflow in the arena and the path from the locker rooms are analyzed to make the playing surface as perfect as possible for the players. This doesn't always work out as planned though. At the 2017 Continental Cup in Las Vegas, it rained the first two days of the event. This precipitation elevated the humidity in the Orleans Arena. Because it doesn't rain often in Las Vegas, the arena doesn't have the dehumidifying equipment that you might see at other facilities. The damp air mixed with the cold surface temperature creating a layer of condensation frost on the ice. Frost slows the rocks down to the point where a shot that might go right to the button ends up ten feet shorter than anticipated. As the game progresses, the frost is worn away in the area where the rocks have been running and the sweepers have been sweeping, and things speed up. However, in spots where the teams haven't played, the ice is still somewhat frosty, the rocks are slower, and reading the ice becomes that much more challenging.

"Dedicated" ice refers to what most people imagine when they think of a curling club. From a rural barn, to a six-sheet curling center with a bar and restaurant, to Saint Paul Curling Club's historic eight sheets, dedicated ice curling clubs have one thing in common: the ice is only for curling. My home club is a converted partially air-cooled hockey arena that was built in Saint Paul during the 1970's. Ultimately, as the hockey players moved to the suburbs, the rink was used less often until it closed. It's been leased for curling only since 2010 but continues to have issues with humidity and air temperature. The Frogtown Curling Club prides itself on being the coldest indoor curling club in America (we haven't exhaustively studied this, but it's unlikely there's a colder one). Where most other clubs are cooled to an air temperature in the 40s, the temperatures on the ice at Frogtown have dipped to the teens. The humidity and cold have a moderate impact on the speed of the ice. Wool socks and fleece underpants are also a must. Americans curling in the Olympics spend the majority of their time curling on the dedicated ice at clubs primarily in Minnesota, Wisconsin, or Washington and only get exposure to championship ice a few times a year.

Unlike Frogtown, which was a hockey facility that was converted to dedicated curling ice, arena ice curlers throw stones in active multi-purpose facilities. Arena ice poses its own set of unique challenges and adventures for curlers because it's typically not as level as dedicated ice. Peaks and valleys in the ice can funnel rocks into channels and force them down a similar path. There might be a ridge the rock just won't climb, no matter how hard you try. At the Oval in Salt Lake, practicing speed skaters can wear down a path on the ice that no general pre-curling maintenance can fully eliminate. During an adventurous game at the La Crosse Curling Club in Wisconsin, we threw a rock down the centerline with an in-turn curl. Normally you would expect this rock to end up on the outside of the twelve-foot (the outermost of the three circles in the house). Instead, the curl of the stone held the rock on a ridge and carried it straight down the ice to the button. Of course, we didn't figure this out until well into the game but mastering out how rocks behave on arena ice is a unique challenge.

Outdoor curling is the way the Scots intended curling to be played, and we know that because it's absolutely miserable. Outdoor curling is usually played during the coldest weekends of the year. Players put on every piece of clothing they own, down a healthy portion of Fireball, then try their hardest to win--or at least not suffer frostbite. Players on outdoor ice aren't using their sliders, as boots will suffice at that temperature and sweeping doesn't help carry the rock. It really is used to move things, such as large cats, out of the way of the stone. The process for outdoor ice making is simpler than any type of indoor ice. First, find a reasonably large body of water and wait for it to freeze. You may be waiting a long time. As the planet gets warmer, there are fewer outdoor bonspiels. To hold rocks and people with all their clothes, you need thick ice and that's happening less and less often even in the areas that once supported outdoor curling. The winter season in Minnesota seems to start with, "Area man on ATV falls through the ice" later and later each year and outdoor bonspiels seem to be fewer and farther between.

CALLING A SHOT

To call a curling shot, the skip places the broom head on the ice with the pad facing up to give the shooter an easy to see target. In baseball, when a pitcher throws a breaking ball, the catcher holds the target where the ball should end up (assuming it's not me in college where the ball would end up somewhere over the outfield fence). The pitcher then determines where to release the ball to curve to the mitt. Curling is different--when a skip puts the broom down on the ice to call a shot, the skip first taps the space on the ice where the rock should end up but then places the broom head in a different location, which is where the thrower aims, not where the rock is supposed to finish. Since the rock curls, the skip needs to consider how heavily a rock should be thrown and how far it will curl. Then they move their broom to where they think the shot should be aimed to achieve the intended goal. If the shooter is drawing to the button, and the ice is getting four to six feet of curl, the broom might be in the middle of the eight-foot (the white center ring) or at the inside edge of the twelve-foot (the outside ring) for the rock to come in and curl to the button. If the shot is a hit, the broom might be an inch or two off the rock, or even on it, depending on how hard the hit has been thrown.

While this seems relatively straightforward, each shooter is different and the behavior of the stone changes as the pebble on the ice wears down during the game. To be successful, skips need to adjust to those changes throughout the game. Occasionally, the player throwing may also have an opinion on where the broom should be for their shot. A brief negotiation period ensues until one player concedes or pretends not to hear the other.

My favorite trick is to move the broom and inch or two to satisfy the shooter, and then when they look down at the rock, move it back. This doesn't always work, but the key is for both the skip and the player shooting to feel comfortable with the shot called. No matter where the rock is expected to end up, that target on the ice is called "broom." As in, "I didn't give you enough broom" when a rock curls further than its intended finishing point and the skip determines they called the shot incorrectly. Or, "You missed it by the amount you were off the broom," as a friend of ours told his wife during a game, to illustrate that she missed the shot by the exact amount she threw wide of the broom, and to signal his intention to sleep on the couch that night.

Along with the placing the broom head on the ice, a skip may choose to extend their right or left arm out as a reminder of which way the shot should curl. If the broom is on the edge of the eight-foot to the right of the skip and they want the shooter to curl to the button, they'll stick out their left hand as if to signal, "curl the rock toward my gloriously extended fingers" or something like that. Although in Canada the hand signals are reversed, or so I'm told, making the United States the Canadian Upside Down which, if you've watched *Stranger Things*, makes total sense on multiple levels. When multiple noisy games are being played simultaneously, skips may also use hand signals to specify weight to the shooter. Touching the elbow signifies normal takeout weight, the wrist for control, or down weight, and the shoulder for firm, or up weight. Finally, if they pat the top of their head they are asking for peel weight and if they rub their belly at the same time, they are just showing off.

For draws and guards, the broom is almost always placed along the tee line. This is to provide perspective for the shooter. Since the tee line doesn't move during the game (as it's painted under the ice) when a rock should be just outside the house the shooter understands that it needs to stop six or seven feet short of where the broom is held. If the target is the button, then the shooter knows the exact weight. Nearly everything in curling is about creating a reference point in comparison to everything else in the game and setting the broom at a fixed distance on the tee line sets a very specific way to measure the shot. Hits, however, are placed on the same plane as the rock to be struck. Since where the rock would end on the shot were it untouched is inconsequential, creating a reference point that is aligned with the stone is beneficial. In all cases when a hit is called, the rock is the end point of the shot and should be treated as such. This is true no matter where the shot stone is called to end up, its unobstructed forward movement stops at the stone it strikes and placing the broom parallel with the rock makes sense.

Once the shooter delivers the stone, *everybody panics and starts yelling!* Actually, this isn't quite true although it may seem like it. The skip is in charge of calling the line, or the curling path the rock is traveling. Quite often the shooter helps with this line call whether it's appropriate or not. The sweepers walk or slide with the rock and determine its weight (how far the rock will travel) and if it will reach the target distance. Rocks may be light (not going to travel far enough) or heavy (going deeper than called). Communication between the sweepers and the skip is important, but where a large portion of the game seems to involve these players all yelling at each other, it's more of a loud negotiation to get the rock where it needs to be.

Sweepers may call out a series of numbers from one to ten to communicate how far they think the rock will carry. This is unironically called the number system. The code is not hard to crack. A one is just past the hog line, two and three are guards outside of the house. Four through six designate spots in the front of the house. Seven is the button. Eight through ten covers the back of the house and "Oh, Crap! Sorry!" is through the house. The number system is another method of bringing tangible points of reference that relate to each other rather than using ambiguous modifiers to describe the gameplay. Once the rock is delivered, one of the sweepers will yell out the number of where they think the rock will end up. This can and will change as the rock moves down the sheet and a six can easily become a three if the rock hits some sticky ice. Or, a sweeper may call a three and then lose their mind from all the vigorous brushing and yell six, only to watch the rock stop a few inches later. It's all relative, and that's the point. The ongoing communication of the skip with the sweepers slowly narrows the gap in understanding about a rock from the time it is released until it comes to a stop.

Next to sweeping, yelling is the part of the game that most entertains the casual observer. Curling is a non-stop conversation from the first rock to the last, punctuated by bouts of skull-shattering commands. "Hurry Hard!" "Sweep!" "On!" "Off!" "Never!" All of these words are instructing the sweepers to either start or stop sweeping. Sweepers are yelling their own information back at the skip. Beer vendors are yelling about beer. Everybody is yelling about the line for the bathrooms. There's a wide variety of words that skips can use or they may string several different guttural utterances together to motivate their sweepers. Generally speaking (yelling), it works fine if the skip is consistent. On a slow draw, I may yell "NEVERNEVERNEVERNEVER—ON!" You might be wondering why I might yell "NEVER!" right before I want my teammates to sweep. It's because no and on sound too much alike and I want them to wait until the exact right moment. Basically, any combinations of words can be used except when "Hard!" is followed in rapid succession with "On!" In that case, it's likely you'll miss the sweep on the shot as everyone in earshot is laughing.

THROWING A STONE

When teaching a learn-to-curl, there isn't a whole lot of time to explain everything beginners might want to know about curling. Since the fundamentals are different from many other sports, it's challenging to cover the necessary information without causing information overload. This often results in instructors reducing curling to its core. Ice is slippery and hard. Don't hurt yourself. Here's the duct tape if you rip the jeans you wore. Just yell random things at your sweepers because no one is listening to you anyway. Have fun and don't break the hacks. The biggest challenge for curlers is bringing together all the separate parts required to properly throw a stone. Since mnemonics are super useful, we teach the ABC's of curling: alignment, balance, and curl. This doesn't always stop people from pushing out of the hack, sliding until they come to a complete stop, then heaving the rock down the ice, but it helps a little.

The process of shooting is as follows: Get your rock and take it to the hack. Clean the bottom of the rock so there isn't any ice or fuzz underneath. Look at the skip to make sure you understand the shot being called. Squat down in the hack making sure your feet and hips are square. Get your broom or stabilizer in place. Give the rock a little spin so it doesn't stick to the ice and stunt your delivery. Pull back slightly with your slider foot while pulling the rock back a hair. Stick your butt up in the air. While making sure your eyes are on the broom, push with the foot in the hack toward the skip's broom. Try not to fall over. Slide on the ice looking at the broom and release the rock with the appropriate handle prior to crossing the hog line. Pop up into your fancy shot-watching squat. Sounds easy, right?

To properly align in the hack, the shooter wants to square his or her hips and feet with a slight (less than an inch) turn toward the broom the skip is holding. This ensures the shooter will push out and slide toward the broom without getting too far off the centerline. Even for a shot at the outermost edges of the twelve-foot, a curler shouldn't come more than a foot or so off the centerline prior to releasing the stone before the hog line. The first time I attempted an out-turn hit from out in the twelve-foot (rotating the rock counterclockwise to curl it from the outside of the house toward the middle), I had a major alignment failure. Not only did I throw the rock out of play, my body came to rest when my face planted firmly in the butt of a curler on the next sheet--much to the surprise and consternation of us both. Alignment is critical as it ensures the stone is thrown on the appropriate line at the broom making sure the curl is predictable. Not putting your face in a stranger's rear end at the end of a shot is an added bonus. Even with a perfectly delivered stone, if the curler's alignment is a centimeter or two off, they'll miss the shot.

Balance is the second key aspect of shooting. If you fall over, the rock isn't going to go very far. You will, however, probably have a really nice bruise to show off at work the next day. When you push out of the hack, the sliding foot should be centered under the middle of your sternum directly behind the rock and lie as flat as possible on the ice to provide the most balance. This is the first point of contact with the ice. A broom or stabilizer in the opposite hand of the rock is the second point of contact. You will see curlers hold their brooms on an angle in front of them, to the side, or even flat on the ice. All three methods provide different points of balance and are likely derived from how the curler learned to throw and what they are comfortable with. The last point of contact is the shooter's trailing foot, which in theory, should be touching the ice with the top side of the toes. The rock isn't used for balance. In reality, the shooting hand is guiding the rock and not relying on it for balance. If a shooter's balance is off and their weight is on top of the stone pressing it down against the ice, this position inevitably requires the shooter to shove the rock and increases the chance of falling on their head once they release the stone.

Most curlers throw with a broom, but some players deliver with a plastic contraption called a stabilizer. These are completely legal at all levels of curling. The stabilizer is simply another method of balancing while throwing a rock and is less wobbly than throwing with the broom. Since the broom's head is much smaller than a stabilizer, it's easy for the arm holding the broom to get wobbly during a throw. Also, because brooms are longer than a stabilizer, more mechanics can be out of alignment if your grip on the broom is too high or too low. The main advantage of learning to throw with the broom first is similar to learning to drive on a manual transmission car. Curlers always have access to a broom, but if they forget their stabilizer or curl at a club that doesn't have them, they will need to be able to curl with a broom. It's also much easier to learn to curl with a stabilizer. If stabilizers are ultimately more effective for curling, then why don't more people use them? First, it's hard to get people to change. Second, it's another piece of equipment to track and can delay the game if they have to keep going to the other end to get it. Third, there's a stigma to using a stabilizer rather than a broom. Finally, why will people get into a ten-car line at the McDonald's drive-thru when there isn't a line inside? I don't know. If you figure it out, let me know and maybe I'll switch to a stabilizer.

The last part of the delivery is the release, but we call it curl because no one would remember the mnemonic ABR unless they were a curling pirate. Typically, the rock is rotated from a 10 o'clock to noon or a 2 o'clock to noon as it is let go. This should generate three to four full rotations of the rock down the ice, generate the appropriate amount of curl, and hit the target. If the rock rotates more than that, it will run straighter down the ice. You may see this, called heavy rotation, intentionally used when throwing a takeout as it helps keep the rock from curling. This sounds counter-intuitive, but the faster the rock spins the longer it takes to catch the pebble on the ice. The opposite of heavy rotation is throwing a rock without any rotation, called no handle or straight handle. A stone with no handle behaves somewhat like a large and slow-moving knuckleball in that it will eventually break one direction or the other, but no one on the ice can predict where it will go.

The principle is that the rock is guided down the ice by the release. Even though we call it throwing a stone, you don't actually throw it anywhere. It's the leg drive out of the hack that should determine the speed of the rock. Some curlers give extra mustard by "pushing" as they release the rock. This is known as a positive release. Sometimes the leg drive out of the hack is too much and a player may feel the need to pull back on the rock to slow it down before they release it. Rarely does a pulled back, or played with, shot reach its intended target, but the result may be better than throwing it through the house.

While all of these principles sound pretty easy and consistent, no two people have the same delivery. A curler like two-time Olympian Jessica Schultz has absolutely no pullback before her delivery; it's more of a quick twitch and she's moving forward with no warning. On the other hand, curling author Guy Schultz (no relation) swings the rock backward in the air and launches his body parallel to the ice. Throwing a curling stone is similar to hitting a baseball in the sense that we can all have a thousand instructional videos advising us what to do, but in the end whatever works best for the individual is what sticks. Some curlers get their upper bodies really low to the ice, while others are more upright when they shoot. It's been argued that people who curl with a more upright body position tend to be better at draws than hits, while those lower to the ice have the opposite skills.

No matter the delivery, the same general principles of alignment, balance, and curl are always in play. The more consistent you are with those three aspects, the closer you will be to hitting your shots.

TYPES OF SHOTS

The following section will discuss the three types of shots curlers throw intentionally and the permutations of those shots that you may hear discussed on television. During my first curling season, I threw two kinds of shots: those that ended in play and those, sadly, that did not. It was incredibly frustrating as I've been reasonably good at most sports, but I just couldn't get the hang of curling right out of the gate. I was having fun, drinking beer and socializing, which was enough to mitigate the steep learning curve of picking up a difficult sport in my thirties. Eight years later I'm still missing a lot of shots, but instead of missing them by feet, I'm often missing by a few inches. Still frustrating, but much more satisfying when I make a really difficult shot that wasn't an accident. A good result for a throw that wasn't the called shot is called Plan B. As in, our original plan for the shot was to do this, but we've adjusted on the fly because the original call just isn't going to work. For example, Plan B may involve a draw to the button that's too heavy, so instead the goal shifts to take out a rock in the back of the house. You may often hear announcers talking about missing on the professional side. This refers to a shot where a couple of things can happen, and the Plan B is discussed outright. If there's a hit to the side of the centerline and the skip yells, "don't be wide," it's likely telling the shooter it's okay to be narrow because other things can happen that wouldn't if it was thrown wide.

Guards

Guards are thrown short of the house to provide cover for rocks in the house. Good teams will throw guards first and then come around (curl behind) the guards with draws into the house. Most of the rest of us accidentally throw a rock in the house, hope our opponent misses hitting it and then try to follow-up with the guard to protect the rock in the house. Strategically, teams with the hammer attempt to start an end with corner guards, i.e. rocks a couple feet in from the side of the sheet and just short of the house that they can throw behind them later in the end. The team without the hammer will try to place a guard directly on the centerline close to the house. This logic is predicated on the belief that it's easier to throw a rock to the button if there's nothing blocking center of the house. The team without the hammer is trying to plug the center up, while the team with the hammer is trying to get one rock behind a corner guard and then draw to the button with the hammer. One of the main rules in curling is the free guard zone, and this is what temporarily protects those early guards from being immediately knocked out of play.

The free guard zone is essentially curling's infield fly rule. The rule makes a lot of sense, but people seem baffled by the concept. Before the free guard zone came into effect, curling was boring: One team would throw a rock, and the other would peel it out. Throw a rock, peel it out. Throw a rock, peel it out. Throw a rock, peel it out. Throw a rock, peel it out. Throw a rock, peel it out. Throw a rock, peel it out. Throw a rock, knock it out for a point. Then some genius presumably woke up from a curling-induced nap sometime around 1990, set down their beer and introduced the idea of the free guard zone. This genius was on Canadian curling great Russ Howard's team and they used a modified free guard zone in practice.

As first introduced, no rock could be knocked out of play until after the leads had thrown all of their stones. This was subsequently modified to the free guard zone rule used today: if any of the first three rocks land in front of the tee line and outside the house (so in the big white area after the hog line, but outside the rings), they can't be knocked out of play until after the fourth rock is thrown. Teams can remove their own stones if they want, but if they hit an opponent's rock and it goes out of play, then that rock is replaced, and the delivered stone is removed from play. In club play, this happens a lot more often than we'd care to admit. With a new curler throwing lead, you can line up a shot called "anywhere in play except hitting the opponent's guard" and inevitably, that rock will travel as if a homing device is aimed to strike the opponent's free guard out.

Hits

The challenge of understanding hit weight calls is because none of them have a logical reference in the natural world, and instead rely on each other for meaning. The order of hit weights from lightest to heaviest is control, normal, firm, and peel. Normal is harder than control but not as heavy as firm, but firm is harder than normal and not as hard as a peel. The other way to define hits by weight is to refer to how far the rock should travel were it not to hit anything. Hack weight means that the rock would make it to the hack before coming to a stop. Board weight means it would go all the way to the back bumper behind the hack. Parking lot weight isn't real curling term but the language I use to describe a pretty heavy rock that's intended to move a bunch of stuff around. You might also hear it referred to "up weight." To simplify, control hits should have the shooter's rock stay in play no matter what. Normal is the shooters standard hit weight and should be thrown in most instances. Firm means a heavier shot that is intended to move more than one rock. Peel is a heavier shot than firm and removes a rock from play while causing the shooter's stone to go out as well.

With control weight, the goal is to hit a rock out and have the shooter's rock stay in play without necessarily hitting the target stone on its center. For a shot to stay in play, it needs to either strike the stationary stone dead center so that it stops at the point of contact (sticking) or hit the rock and roll to another point in the house. In contrast, words such as "skinny," "thin," and "thick" refer to how closely the delivered stone should strike to the center of the stationary rock. Thick means the delivered stone will strike closer to the center of the rock so it has less sideways movement after hitting the stationary target stone. Skinny or thin means the delivered rock will have more movement because it's hitting the stationary stone further from the center. If a house has several guards on the right-hand side, and the opponent has a rock sitting in the four-foot on the left-hand side, a skip can call control weight, to knock the stationary stone out of play to the left while the shooter's rock rolls to the right behind the guards.

Normal weight is the hardest hit weight to quantify but is essentially the "just throw it at a comfortable weight that ensures the struck rock goes out of play and your rock does what we want it to do" weight. If that sounds vague, it is. Most hits in a game are thrown at a normal weight.

Firm weight is where things start to get interesting. That's the weight when players start to experiment with fun sounding things like doubles and triples. Firm weight is thrown with the intent of moving multiple rocks in the house. If the shooter hits a rock and then strikes a different rock and both of those go out of play, that's a double. If the shooter hits one rock and it crashes into another and that stone knocks two other rocks out, that's also double. In any instance, where the shooting team knocks two of the opponent's rocks out, it's called a double. Hit three out and it's a triple. Hit four out and you'll get a lot of views on YouTube.

Peel weight is used in several different instances. The first is when a team's shooter wants to remove a guard from play and prevent the delivered rock from also becoming a guard. The shooter throws peel weight to split the stationary guard out of play in one direction while the ricochet sends the shooter out of play in the other direction. A skip might throw peel weight with the eighth rock of an end to knock out the opponent's rock and their own in order to blank the end (score zero points) and retain the hammer for the next end.

Runbacks and raises are the other two types of hits you'll hear about in curling. Runbacks are heavier weight hits intended to strike a guard or rock in the front of the house sending it back to knock out a rock behind the struck rock. For example, the opposing team might have a rock in the house that's just off center from another rock that is guarding it. The delivering team can throw a runback that hits the guard on the nose and then hits the rock in the house on an angle sending them scurrying out of play in opposite directions. Raises, also called a tap back, are more of a finesse hit. The intent of a raise is to push your own rock back a few feet and into scoring position. This is likely going to be thrown with a control weight because of the chance that tapping the rock with more weight will send it all the way through the back of the house, completely wasting the shot and leaving the team in the same position as prior to throwing the raise. A team with a centerline guard might try to hit it lightly on the nose to push the guard into the eight-foot while replacing it with the shooter's rock as the new guard. A skip may also attempt a raise if there are a lot of guards hanging around the front of the house. In championship level play, those skips will generally draw around the mess of guards and put the shooter close to the pin. For the rest of us, we might choose to bump that rock back as it feels like it's a lot less challenging of a shot, even if it really isn't.

Draws

The hardest shot in curling is drawing to the button with the hammer. Unless you are me, then the hardest shot in curling is drawing anywhere in an empty house for a single point. The rings might be twelve feet in diameter, but when you are standing more than a hundred feet away, the house might as well be half the size of a stone. Draws are shots that are intended to finish somewhere in the house and be a potential scoring rock. A draw could be behind a guard or just out there in the open exposed to all humankind. The point is that rock should come to rest at a designated spot inside the house. Draws require the skill of the shooter with the weight judgment of the sweepers and the line call from the skip or vice-skip. A successful draw is a complete team effort.

A freeze is a draw that is intended to come to rest touching another rock in the house. You get in there, throw the draw and sit on another stone. If the two rocks that are frozen together are hit later in the end, the rock thrown for the freeze doesn't move from the house. It's the same concept as the Newton's Cradle desk toy, the balls swing down and strike the stationary balls, but the struck ball stays in place while the other ones go shooting up into the air on the other end. The same thing happens when you freeze one or more rocks on another one and then hit them later.

The last type of draw you may hear about is one you are unlikely to see. That's the Last Stone Draw. Last stone does not mean the hammer but instead refers to a draw taken during practice ice. Throughout the week of a competitive tournament, players on each team will throw their last practice rocks to the button. These draws are then measured for the distance from the pin. The total distance is tallied up and the team with the lower score will get the hammer to start the game. For those of us who need a yardstick to measure our draws to the button, we just flip a coin and the winner takes the hammer and the loser picks a color. In beer league play, extra ends may be decided by a last stone draw (sometimes called last shot draw) from the skips or a four-rock end, depending on how much time is left before the next league starts.

RULES AND ETIQUETTE

A t its heart, curling is a very simple game. The United States Curling Association rulebook is a short fifty-two pages, but only ten of those pages are dedicated to the rules of gameplay (by comparison, the 2015 Major League Baseball rulebook clocks in at a whopping 282 pages) and can easily be polished off in one eventful bathroom trip. The rest of the rulebook is focused on rules for championship level play, what can be on your uniform, and who needs to pay for what. Nearly all the actual in-game of curling rules amount to "The skips will figure it out and come to an agreement."

There are officials in curling, but they are typically focused on timing the game and watching for hog line violations when the appropriate technology is not available. What they don't do is sit on-high like a tennis umpire and make calls. They don't need a chest protector and mask even though getting hit with a lively curling stone might hurt. Since curling has few rules, there's not a lot of need for arcane interpretation of rules. As far as I can tell, and I did spend two full days in officiating classes, the primary responsibility of the official when there is an on-ice dispute is to say, "I don't know, what do you two think?" while looking thoughtful in a black turtleneck.

Recently, I went to sweep a rock out of the back of the house, slipped and fell on top of it. My opposing skip said, "It was going out anyway" and we took it off the ice. Not "Well, a spider could have frozen to death in the rafters and dropped immediately in front of the rock stopping its movement, so we should probably put it in the back twelve." In the same game, we had a perfect draw coming right to the button. Our two sweepers bumped brooms and the lead sweeper hit the stone and burned it. She immediately stopped the rock and pulled it from play. I was fewer than six feet from the infraction and didn't even realize it had happened. But that's one of the things that make curling special. It's rare that you need to police an opponent or that a play is so controversial that it creates bad blood. However, it can happen and without officials interfering with the guiding principle that the skips should ultimately decide, there can be some unpleasantness.

In the 2016 Men's World Championship, Team USA was playing Team Japan in a qualifying game. Team Japan's skip threw a takeout. It struck a rock, caromed off the sideboard, struck another moving rock still in play and bumped it away from the house. In a perfect world, the shooter would have been caught as soon as it touched the sideboard, and there wouldn't have been a disagreement about the placement of Team USA's rock. Because the infraction was committed by Team Japan, the United States team had the final say in how the rock should be placed. Ultimately, Team USA insisted the rock be placed in the house and then threw the hammer to score three and went on to win the game 5-4. After watching the replay several times, I wouldn't want to be the person responsible for placing that rock. Imagine Italy and Brazil playing a World Cup match and each team's captain had to agree if a player took a dive in the box or if a penalty kick should be awarded. The crowd would get to watch about eight minutes of soccer and eighty-two minutes of dramatic lobbying. In this case, nothing was going to happen until the skips came to an agreement about the play. While the fans and some players were particularly disgruntled about it, an official was not going to step in and place that stone. The teaching moment here is that if you don't want to make tough decisions, sweepers should catch the rocks, but the players deciding the outcome of a controversial play is very different from other sports.

Since the official rules are scant, the unwritten rules of curling are the driving force for the game and are known as etiquette. This can be exceedingly stressful for a new curler. Surprisingly, a number of these "unwritten rules" are often printed out on posters in 28-point font, which makes them written unwritten rules.

For the most part, etiquette involves common sense and general politeness. Show up on time. Shake hands with your opponents and wish them "good curling" before the game. Don't cheer your opponent's misses. Winning team cleans the ice. Things like that.

Other stuff isn't written down. It's rude to walk down the sheet when someone is shooting. Don't try to speed up the game by setting your opponent's rock by the hack for them. Spend at least thirty minutes sitting with your opponent after the game. If it's mathematically impossible for you to win the game, known as being run out of rocks, you should offer your hand to the opponent and concede. When a team is shooting, the opposing players should either be behind the houses or between the hog lines when the shot is being delivered and generally still. Otherwise, it's considered very rude.

For experienced curlers, this stuff seems like common sense, but when you are new to curling and focused on not falling over on the ice and dying, it can be a little much for the brain to handle, and breaches can happen early and often. It's important to provide a comfortable environment for new curlers while also making them aware of the inadvertent things they are doing that might drive other players crazy.

Here's where that gets difficult. Skips should communicate etiquette violations between each other and then the skips address the issue with the offending player. It's not like there's an official out there throwing a yellow flag to handle this stuff. For a player who is already confused simply learning how to curl, to get negative feedback from their skip about an honest mistake can be very disheartening. It's a fine line to walk. It is the difference between trying to teach someone everything at once and understanding there are going to be unwritten rules that people just aren't aware of or things they have been told but haven't yet stuck because they are desperately trying not to slip and fall on the hard ice.

At the competitive level, breaches of etiquette are infrequent but when they do make the news it is a massive production. At the Brier in 2015, a million Canadian think pieces were spawned when Northern Ontario curler E.J. Harnden tapped Mark Kean from regular old Ontario on his shoe while he was watching his rock go down the ice. Curlers don't practice their rock watching pose. At least I hope they don't. Instead, it evolves over time. For example, my shot watching pose is less crouched down holding my broom like a staff, and more of a "please god let me hit the shot and not fall over, okay I can fall over if I hit the shot." The incident at the Brier involved two different etiquette breaches. Kean was guilty of leaving his knee down on the ice for too long, which can melt the surface and cause problems later in the game. The second breach was Harden's use of his broom to tap an opposing player as a reminder to not puddle the ice. This was the big no-no. There should never be physical contact between opposing players unless it's accidental. Instead of hitting him on the shoe, Harden should have said something to his skip or complained to the officials. In this instance, an official can warn the player and eject them if the behavior continues. So, it turns out curling officials can do something during curling matches after all. I take back everything I said earlier.

CURLING STONES

If you were sporting a balaclava and looking around the inside of a curling club for something to permanently borrow, pound for pound the most valuable items are the curling stones. While probably not the easiest thing to take in a smash and grab, at around $11,000 for a set of sixteen, each pound carried off is worth about $16. Funds at most curling clubs are tight, so the loss of even one stone can be a huge pain. At the 2015 Lake Bemidji Winterfest, curlers took to the outdoor ice for the first time since the 1930s. By all accounts it was a successful bonspiel, but for one problem. The guy in charge of counting the rocks at the end had 95 and you don't need all your fingers and toes to know that 95 isn't divisible by eight. Someone had involuntarily liberated one of the stones from the event.

Now, these stones weren't owned by the Lake Bemidji Winterfest, they were borrowed from the Crookston Curling Club and were needed for the league on Monday night. While it's unusual to have fifteen rocks in play when it's time to throw the hammer, you also don't want to take a chance on playing, "Ghost rock on the button." Curlers, being the loose-walleted and generous people that they are, quickly raised $280 of the $500 needed to get a replacement and had one shipped from Winnipeg for an extra $82. The stolen stone was reunited with its set a few weeks later when it was found on the doorstep of the Bemidji Curling Club with a note of apology taped to it. "Thought this belongs back here. Sorry, didn't mean to cause such an inconvenience. Hopefully, there wasn't too much trouble. – Sorry Citizen." While Crookston got a happy ending where the kidnapped stone ended up back with its friends, it cost the Winterfest committee international shipping and a whole lot of trouble. Please don't get into the black-market curling stone business.

The reason curling stones are so expensive and cause such a hassle when one is stolen, lost, or broken is that they are not made from just any old granite. Curling stones are made from granite quarried from one place in the world, an island off the coast of Scotland called Ailsa Craig. The island is the remaining plug from an extinct volcano and its granite contains a low amount of quartz, and so the structure of the rock is tighter. This composition prevents moisture from getting inside the granite where it can freeze and expand. The process of freezing and expanding repeats itself in curling stones made of normal granite until the stone degrades and it chips or, more excitedly, breaks. Breaking a stone is unusual, but it can happen. The Saint Paul Curling Club has a quite jagged and festive doorstop made from a broken rock. I'm likely never to see a stone break in my lifetime, but if I do, the USCA handbook has explicit instructions on how to handle that situation. The skips will figure it out and if they can't, teams will have to replay the end.

There are two parts to the granite of the curling stone, and both come from Ailsa Craig. Blue Hone is used for the running band, the part of the rock that glides on the ice, and Common Green is used for the center of the stone called the striking band. The running band is the part of the rock that has contact with the surface of the ice when the rock is thrown. It's not particularly big: just a little over two inches in width. The striking band is the rest of the stone that makes a satisfying "thwump!" when it encounters other stones and is the part that also bruises your big toe when you stop it with your foot.

Now you might be wondering, "Why can't they just mine more of this special granite to create more curling stones?" Well, it turns out that the island is a protected bird sanctuary. This means every decade or so, Kays of Scotland (who has exclusive rights to the granite) can go in and collect granite that is freely available. Their last haul off the island gave them enough granite to make stones until 2020. I can't speak to how many curling stones are sold each year, but I can't imagine it's many. Hard-to-destroy curling stones aren't particularly a growth industry unless people keep stealing them.

Rock handles are usually red and yellow, but there's no reason they can't be other colors that don't look the same to a colorblind player. They are plastic and bolted to the rock. It's important to note that there isn't a top and bottom to a curling stone, the handle can be screwed into either end of the stone. If you are watching the Olympics in high definition, you may notice letters and numbers of the rocks. Because there are a lot of orderly people in the world, rocks typically will have four characters on them: two designating the sheet to which they belong (A, B, C, D) and two designating a number (1, 2, 3, 4, 5, 6, 7, 8). A rock that has C and 3 on it would be located on sheet C and would typically be the third rock thrown by a team in an end. However, the curling rules don't require players to follow the number order on the rocks. The number is a reference for the curlers to distinguish it from the other rocks on the sheet. You could probably call the rocks Jayden and Kaitlynn, but that would be annoying for those of us who aren't millennials.

The problem with the need for order and structure in life is that when it comes time to clean the rocks from the house after an end, people feel compelled to put them in order rather than grabbing the appropriate rocks when their time comes to throw. For argument's sake, let's say organizing rocks takes 90 seconds each end. By the start of the eighth end of the game, ten and a half minutes have been spent organizing rocks out of 120 minutes of game time. That's nearly ten percent of the time recreational curlers have to play and that seriously cuts into our beer drinking. For competitive curlers, that cuts into thinking time. At the Frogtown Curling Club, the managers ran an experiment where they replaced the numbers with, get this, more letters, so there were no numbers on the rocks at all. Those first few weeks were mayhem, like people running in the streets while a supervillain decimated Manhattan, but after a brief adjustment period, we all learned to curl without numbers, saved some time each game, and learned a little bit about ourselves in the process.

Clubs make money by selling names on the handles of rocks. It also becomes a source of fun and money. I skipped a game at the Saint Paul Curling Club where a friend of mine sponsored a rock. I sent him a text after the game. "I threw your yellow 8 last night. Terrible rock. You should request a refund." I always do this when throwing a sponsored rock of someone I know, but I didn't expect the following response. "It is a cutter, that's why I had picked it up. FYI, I never choose yellow rocks on that sheet and when you do have them, never throw seven and eight." I replied that I was just kidding and got back, "There is no messing with the truth, that rock is a cutter," in reply. Please note that I have not disclosed the name of the person from the conversation nor what sheet it is at Saint Paul. Since the rocks and configuration are not likely to change anytime soon, I need to hold any advantage I can, even if it's just psychological.

If you are watching the Olympics, you might also notice little colored lights on the rocks, generally green, but maybe red if the curler has screwed up. This fancy technology is called Eye on the Hog and is used to monitor hog line infractions. Like Jell-O, Eye on the Hog is the name of a product. The generic term is an electronic hog line monitoring device, which is both vague and significantly less fun than Eye on the Hog. No matter where you are reading this right now, just belt out "Suuueee! Eye on the Hog!" See, it's a lot of fun. Remember, the shooter needs to completely release the stone before the hog line for it to be a legal throw and the Eye on the Hog tracks this.

Self-management of the rules is a real challenge for hog line violations, either because throwers are so focused on the target that they don't realize they've committed a hog line violation, or they are just unethical. It's hard to call your own hog line violation fairly. Having your opponent call it is unreasonable as well. If they aren't standing on the hog line, their angle of perception is off except for the most blatant violations. BYOHVC (bring your own hog line violation calls) were eventually replaced in competitive events with officials who stood at the hog line at the end of all the sheets and were tasked with watching every shot for a hog line violation. Curling officials, at least in the United States, are volunteers. "Hey buddy, wear your black turtleneck. Here's a heavy coat. Go stand out there and watch someone throwing from fifty yards away and let us know if they cross the hog line with three other games in the way." Not exciting or effective.

Finally, the geniuses at Startco Engineering Ltd. invented the "Eye on the Hog." Curling clubs now embed a strip of metal in the hog line running the length of the ice. The stone has a magnetic sensor in the handle so that when it crosses the path of the metal strip and there's no hand on it, the rock will light up green. If an ungloved hand is still attached to the rock, it will light up red to signal the hog line violation and the rock is pulled from play.

EQUIPMENT

The great thing about curling is that you don't have to own any specialized equipment prior to trying the game your first time. All you need is to put on a hat, warm socks, and clean shoes and show up at the curling club or arena. Every club stocks the essentials that new curlers need, like rocks, brooms, sliders, and ibuprofen. Brand new curlers can throw some stones, sweep a little, and try really hard not to concuss themselves.

Much like every other adult recreational activity, new curlers slowly start to collect gear as they continue to play. A broom purchase at their first bonspiel. Making their own curling shoes. Buying another broom that more expresses their individuality. Then one day they have shoes, dedicated pants, socks, hat, screwdrivers, duct tape (black), a stopwatch, whiskey and everything else needed to fill up a gym bag and not have room for anything more. New curlers don't amass all of this equipment at once, but there are some major purchases that make you feel like a "curler."

Brooms

Once the addiction to curling begins to set in, the first purchase novice curlers often make is a broom. It's a thrill to no longer have to use a heavy old club broom and start to play with a fancy multicolored carbon fiber brush with a shiny new pad. I'll never forget buying my first broom, which is a surprise since I'd consumed multiple Irish coffees in the hours leading up to the purchase. It was the Saturday morning of our first ever bonspiel, and it sat on the shelf, black and green and much lighter, shinier and fancier than the wood club broom with its pillow sized pad I'd used for my entire first season. The shiny new broom was eighty dollars and

I had two more games to curl. How could I not buy that broom? It's almost as if the credit card was controlling my fingers, willing itself out of my wallet to get me that broom. That broom now sits in my basement, lonely and sad as I have replaced it with another, even more expensive broom. Most curlers have similar stories.

The purpose of a broom, as everyone is told at their first learn-to-curl event, is to heat the ice in front of the rock which briefly melts the pebble. This melting causes the rock to travel further and straighter by reducing the friction. I won't (or can't) get into the physics of this, so all you need to know is that this works like magic. Brooms have been an integral part of curling since the sport started. Originally, Scottish curlers used brooms from their home to sweep snow, ice, small bits of haggis, and the occasional wayward kilt out from in front of the path of the stone. As curling progressed from pastime to sport, corn bristled brooms were used and slapped on the ice making a satisfying "Thwap! Thwap! Thwap!" as the sweepers moved down the ice. Corn brooms quickly wore out or damaged from all the thwapping, so as a result players would often go through multiple brooms in a bonspiel weekend. Corn brooms gave way to wood or plastic handled brooms with solid, fixed heads and bristles made of hair. Broom heads then evolved into the synthetic ones you see today with broom handles made of a carbon fiber mix. Today's brooms have flexible heads, which provide different angles for throwing, sweeping or calling a shot.

You may notice during the Olympics, or any other major event that curlers may have different broom designs, but all of them have the same colored broom pad. That color is officially known as Mustard Yellow Oxford 420D, which sounds like a banned food coloring. This standardization resulted from a controversy that swept (puns!) through the curling world in 2015.

The controversy was called "Broomgate," and it came to a head because of a broom released a few years earlier. Hardline Curling invented a new broom called the "Ice Pad." There wasn't anything particularly special about it until Hardline had the cash to sponsor some elite teams who had the sweeping skill to take advantage of the broom. Those curlers figured out how to make the rock they were sweeping do some magical things with this new technology. While it's been described by the CBC and others as controlling a stone with a joystick, in truth it wasn't that dramatic. However, with appropriate sweeping techniques, curlers could make a stone move against its curl by three to four feet or even slow a rock down. The sweeping technique in conjunction with certain fabrics and inserts inside the pad scratched the ice rather than just melting the pebble causing rocks to move in an unexpected way.

There were a number of arguments from the curling community about whether this was detrimental to the game.

First, traditionalists argued that the point of making a shot was on the shooter and not technology that allowed sweepers to make a bad shot successful. Imagine a baseball bat that had a homing device in it that reduced strikeouts and increased contact. Second, these traditionalists argued that the reliance on technology meant that players with the money to buy this equipment had a distinct advantage over those who didn't. Third, there was a fear that a technology arms (or brooms) race would hurt curling in the long run by focusing on advanced equipment rather than the skill of the shooter. Finally, and perhaps most importantly, was the concern that the use of these brooms was damaging the ice by scratching and changing the playing surface.

These concerns led to a broom summit where the Canadian government helped coordinate scientists and curlers to get to the bottom of what was going on and to recommend appropriate technology changes. Ultimately, the group standardized on Mustard Yellow Oxford 420D fabric for the broom pads. Scientists sampled numerous different fabrics in a myriad of configurations to analyze their impact on the ice surface. They even tested whether different colored broom pads had an effect, but the results were inconclusive. They ultimately recommend only one color for broom heads just in case. Broomgate changed the way curlers swept with the new technology, and many of those changes have continued after the standardization of broom pads.

Even today, curlers are still allowed to use whatever brooms they would like when they throw, so you'll see shooters using a wide variety of brooms that don't look nearly as fancy as what they use to sweep. For example, you may see excessively taped up rocket shaped brooms. These are old corn brooms pulled up from grandpappy's basement, duct taped back together and used for throwing. On one hand, it's neat to see those old brooms again, on the other hand, they tend to get corn strands all over the ice and can make a bit of a mess.

Shoes

Cleveland is a northern town, but its rainy winter weather and lack of hills mean it's not conducive to winter sports other than drinking beer and commiserating about the Browns. As a Cleveland native, that's my burden to bear. As a curler, it means I'll never be "gliding backward gracefully on my slider as I cock my head to the right and thoughtfully consider my shot" cool, but that's probably okay since I've mostly mastered not killing myself by falling on the ice. There are tradeoffs in life and being alive is generally better than being cool. Also, stay in school, kids.

If not bought in conjunction with a broom, curling shoes are typically the next thing a new curler purchases. Besides the standard features of shoes, curling shoes have several specialized parts to them. These include a slider, grippers, toe coat and if you are fancy, lace covers. For the average curler, the first time they step out on the ice, they don't have fancy curling shoes. Every club has a box of scratched up Teflon sliders that are either step-on or the more festively named strap-on sliders to be used with their regular shoes. While sweeping is actually much more dangerous than sliding, sliding out of the hack to deliver your first stone is the most terrifying part of the first curling experience. "You want me to bend over, stick my butt in the air and slide down the ice with that thing? I'd rather jump out of a plane." The reality is that you can't fall very far on a detached slider, and if you wipe out, you're close to the ground. If you try to stand up with a step-on slider after delivering the stone, there is more risk of falling, but generally, at most you'd ever get is bruised knee.

As a curler's level of interest in the game and their bravery increases, the desire for curling shoes goes up exponentially. My first pair were some Converse Chuck Taylors sitting in the closet that I didn't ever wear. I bought a slider kit, which is just a piece of Teflon coated plastic, jaggedly cut it in the shape on my shoe, glued it on and then left it under a stack of my wife's law school books for a few weeks (except for the one we used to keep a couch away from the wall, this was the last time these books were used for anything). I loved my homemade shoes, but eventually, I upgraded to a pair of professionally customized Chucks, and then when I wore those out, I had a pair of Adidas made into curling shoes. While I'm on my third pair of dedicated curling shoes, I've never owned actual curling shoes made by a curling shoe manufacturer. Wading through the myriad of options can be paralyzing, and it's like shopping for a grill. You look at the eighty-dollar grill and it's nice, but the ninety-five dollar one is a little better. Next thing you know, it's five hours later you've made it to the end of the grills only to discover you are purchasing a Churrascaria in Omaha.

As mentioned above, brooms are often the first thing new curlers purchase because they come in lots of festive colors and even the best on the market are significantly cheaper than shoes. In contrast, curling shoes are both boring and expensive. Shoes from a manufacturer are just like a Model-T, you can have them in any color you want as long as it's black. Shoes, unlike brooms also don't have to fit. This is a huge problem for curling in the United States. As you might guess, there isn't a massive market for curling supplies in the United States, so you just can't waddle down to the nearest Dick's Sporting Goods to try on a pair. You can't really test them out either because as soon as you step on the ice with a pair, they are then "used" and can't be returned. A few years ago, I excitedly purchased my wife a pair of shoes as a gift. She tried them on and they fit. Score one for the good guys. She got to the club and found that the slider was designed in a way that didn't work with her delivery. When she would start forward, the end of the slider would catch the ice, dig into it, and chip it. After a few games, we gave the shoes to a friend. I think they are now sitting in a box, in a bag of curling gear, in the New York-New Jersey-Pennsylvania metro area waiting to get used again.

On a whim, I called a major curling supplies manufacturer and asked if they had a stock of defective or damaged shoe inventory. The typical sort of write-down equipment that most manufacturers would have. Their response was a strong no, which surprised me. Their first move was to ask if we wanted to sell their product (also strong no on my side as the value of inventory carried to revenue isn't particularly compelling), and then they suggested I work with a reseller either three hours north or in an adjacent state. I'm not suggesting that it's easier to buy a canoe in Arizona (fun fact, 0.3% of the state is water) than it is to buy curling shoes in the Twin Cities, but it's probably close.

Next to the challenging return policy, the strangest part about buying curling shoes is that you purchase either right or left-handed shoes. Even NFL kickers, who often wear different shoes on each foot, are making that decision on footedness rather than handedness. Different bits go in different places on the shoe depending on which hand a player throws with. For a right-handed shooter, the left foot has the slider on it and the right foot gets a gripper and a toe coat. To visualize, a right-handed shooter pushes out of the hack with their right hand on the stone and they slide on their left foot. The right foot, the one that was in the hack, trails behind with the top of the foot-dragging on the ice. Each part of the curling shoe needs to be on the correct foot for this all to work properly.

Most of the differences in curling shoe technology relate to the slider. The thickness of the slider and the stiffness of the shoe's sole are the most important components that can affect the sliding process. There are a million and one unique ways people slide, but the general rule of thumb is that a thicker slider and a stiffer sole is better for sliding on the ice. Along with your foot, the sole and slider move different ways as you slide out of the hack. The movement of all three creates instability and impacts the shooter's balance. As the slider gets thicker, there's less wobble side-to-side as the foot compensates for the movement of the slider. Think about Ralphie's little brother in *A Christmas Story* with all those thick clothes on—he can't move his arms. This is a much more stable environment than if he were just wearing a t-shirt and shivering all over the place. Now, there's a limit to these general principles; you couldn't take a pair of wedge heels and slap on a slider and be the most stable person on the ice. Curling shoes tend to max out at a quarter inch thick slider. These can either be a full solid piece under the shoe or discs on the ball and heel of the shoe.

The sliders are the most complex part of the shoe, but if you ask me, grippers are the most key feature. On the throwing hand, the sole of the shoe has rubber material attached that helps it grip the ice when you walk. For the sliding foot, what amounts to a mini-galosh (is there a singular for galoshes?) goes over the shoe to cover the slider when a player isn't shooting. When watching the Olympics, grippers are the black thingies people are regularly tossing around the ice. These may have been called rubbers in other contexts, but I don't want to confuse anyone under the age of 106.

Many of the more skilled curlers, or those with a death wish, play the entire game without ever putting that gripper over their slider. This is deemed particularly helpful when sweeping takeouts as you can more easily keep up with the swift-moving rock. For guards and draws, slider sweeping isn't as effective because you cannot put as much pressure on the ice. Also, it's dangerous. As someone who finds themselves suddenly and unexpectedly accelerating to the ground at an unpleasant rate on dry land, sweeping on my slider is too dangerous for me.

Another part of the curling shoe is the toe coat. The trailing foot, the same side as the throwing hand, drags on the ice during the delivery slowing the curler down. Putting a shiny coat of resin over the toe of the trailing shoe reduces that drag. It also can surprise the crap out of you the first time you throw with a toe coat because the increased speed out of the hack will exaggerate any flaws in your delivery.

The last unique part of curling shoes is a lace cover. This is a band of shoe material that Velcros over the laces and provides no discernable value, like a rearview mirror in a car. Lace covers may reduce drag on the trailing shoe a little bit and for a mere forty dollars can save you maybe only maybe six dollars of shoelaces over the life of the shoe. So, there's that.

Pants

Do not wear jeans to curl in. Before you learn about ice safety, balance, or which end of the broom to put on the ice, you should learn not to wear jeans while curling. Technically, you can curl in jeans, but it's not a good idea because you're likely to split your pants, and then you have to buy new skinny jeans. Personally, I've had people ignore this very strong recommendation and end up having to use a roll of duct tape to keep their boy or girl parts from being exposed to everyone on the ice. Your first-time curling is very stressful. You learn to sweep and get the general gist of throwing the rock. As the event progresses you get more comfortable, start to stretch out to better throwing form, and then you hear fabric tearing as your jeans rip from crotch to thigh. Suddenly, you feel a whole bunch of fresh skin being introduced to the cold air. Don't wear jeans to curl in.

The ultimate question I had to ask myself as I started this book was "Do I have to write about the Norwegian men's curling pants?" And of course, as a primer for people who might be watching curling in the Olympics, the answer is yes. The first step is to clarify that it's Team Ulsrud's festive pants, and not specifically Team Norway's festive pants. It's not like the official governing body said, "You know what our curling teams need? Colorful pants!" For a decade, Thomas Ulsrud has skipped the Norwegian men's team in international play. In 2008 and 2012, Team Ulsrud's pantwear captured the attention of curling fans everywhere. It apparently started as an accident, when the team didn't get the correct uniform during the run-up to the Vancouver Olympics. One of the team members was looking for golf pants, as they are stretchy enough for curling and work quite well if you don't want regular old curling pants (Note: Jeans were never considered as a replacement). Instead of black, they ordered red, white and blue checked golf pants from a California company named Loudmouth, and I think you can see where this is going: The pants were loud. They turned out to be a hit, so much so that during the Olympics, Loudmouth's servers crashed from people shopping for their pants—the Air Jordans of the curling world. Curling fashion is designed to blend into the background, like a solid colored Waldo, but Team Ulsrud took curling's fun from the post-game watering hole and put it on display for everyone to see. In 2017, Team Walstad represented Norway at the Men's World Championships and wore traditional black curling pants, which wasn't nearly as fun.

This did send the curling blogosphere a twitter as questions about their legality came into play. To be fair, loud pants can be a distraction for a curler, but I'd argue it's less of a distraction than a 350-pound defensive lineman in a Nike color rush uniform. But no, the pants don't break any rules at the international level. They simply must be approved by the IOC prior to use, and there's nothing wrong with adding a little color to the game. In sad news for Team Walstad, but fantastic news for us, Team Ulsrud will be representing Norway at the 2018 Winter Olympics with a new round of exciting pants.

Gloves

Wearing gloves for curling makes sense because it's cold, right? Vigorously brushing the ice can also lead to wear and tear on your hands, so gloves provide a significant amount of protection. You might ask why curlers on TV are uni-gloved like a Michael Jackson video when it comes time to deliver a stone. It's not because removing the glove provides some inherent tactile advantage. Baseball players wear batting gloves, even some NFL quarterbacks wear a glove on their throwing hand, but there's a technological reason why curlers remove the glove on their throwing hand--electronic hog line monitoring devices. Non-competitive curlers, such as myself, don't have to worry about products like the Eye on the Hog because they aren't used at most clubs for league night. I can wear six gloves on my right hand and do a finger puppet reenactment of *Stranger Things* if I want to (and I really want to), but elite curlers don't get to have that kind of fun.

The Eye on the Hog monitors each shot for hog line violations and it requires the touch of human flesh on the handle to activate it. Tilting the rock to clean it, a special skill that takes time a long time to master, with a bare hand activates the sensor in the handle and turns the lights green. If the rock is released prior to the hog line, the lights stay green. If the hand is still in contact with the handle as the rock crosses the magnetic strip embedded in the ice, the lights turn red and you have a hog line violation. This doesn't function properly if you are wearing a glove, which if you ask me, is a bug and not a feature.

And that's really all there is to say about gloves. Except, maybe, that some curlers wear leather mittens which isn't as nearly bad-ass as you might think.

Stopwatches

It's surprising how much stopwatches are used in curling given that gameplay lasts for a couple of hours and thankfully there's no sprinting as that's a Summer Olympics sport. The skips and sweepers all use stopwatches during a match to time different aspects of a delivered stone and then convert that time into weight or distance. It's not like there's a metaphorical Excel spreadsheet in each player's head where they are constantly calculating formulas, but rather stopwatches are used to inform sweepers as part of split-second decisions and to guide skips in determining how to call shots.

There are two types of stopwatches you'll see on the curling sheet. The first is the traditional stopwatch looped around a belt that you'll see bouncing around players are throwing or sweeping. The second type is designed to be Velcroed to the broom handle. Regardless of which type is used, the function of the stopwatch is the same--to get a general understanding of the speed of the ice and act as a guide to the sweepers to let them know if they need to sweep the rock for weight. If you are thinking, "Great, this sounds like it makes sweeping so much easier," understand that there are a billion and one caveats to using a stopwatch. Timing a rock isn't an exact science. It's more of a 10-day forecast rather than traffic and weather on the tens. Every delivery is different and ice changes from end-to-end and even rock-to-rock. Relying on only the stopwatch to determine if you should sweep for weight will likely cause more harm than watching it with your eye or getting a sense of the speed of the rock while you travel down the ice next to it.

Several factors affect the distance a shot travels and therefore affect the timing of a rock. If you're playing the first game on a sheet that day, the ice may be frosty, but as the frost wears off the ice, the rocks will speed up. Toward the end of the game, the pebble will wear down reducing friction and some tracks on the ice may be faster than others. Throwing the rock with more rotation causes it to go further. Delivering with a positive release (or releasing the stone with a slight push) rather than naturally releasing it will cause it to travel further. All this adds up to mean that my 3.86 split time from end line to hog line is not the same as your 3.86, nor is my 3.86 the same 3.86 the next time I throw a rock.

If timing is so unreliable, why do it? While it does aid in making split-second sweeping decisions, timing also creates a common language for the team to use. Adjectives like fast and slow don't have a granular enough meaning for effective communication. "Faster than normal" sounds like it's helpful, but if that can't be placed in a relatable context, it isn't particularly useful. Does faster than normal mean I need to write a novella between the time I push out of a hack and finally release the stone? Or is it just a hair slower than normal draw weight? By using time, we can fine tune our adjectives. Let's continue to use 3.86 as a guide. In the second end, I throw a 3.86 and it lands at the top of the four-foot without sweeping. That doesn't mean the exact same thing will happen in the eighth end, but what it tells the shooter is that 3.86 is a pretty good time if you want your sweepers to carry it to the button. If I come out slow and throw a 4.1, they have a good sense that they might need to jump on the rock quickly. If I were to throw a 3.6, they might want to wait a little longer and visually analyze how the rock is doing before sweeping. In either case, timing the rock provides a fifth set of eyes on the shot to help fine tune what each player is thinking.

There are three ways curlers can time a rock. In the first, the sweepers start timing during the delivery when the rock crosses the backline and stops the watch when the rock crosses the near hog line (the 3.86 discussed above). Interval timing may also take place from the tee line to the hog line as this flattens the differences in delivery between players. Interval timing assists the sweepers in judging the speed of the rock for draws when they should sweep. Assuming the shooter's delivery is relatively consistent, a number in the ballpark of previous numbers will help confirm what the sweepers are observing about the weight of the rock. Interval timing is useful for draws and guards but does not provide guidance for a takeout.

The second method is to time from hog line to hog line. This method won't help a sweeper to decide to start sweeping a rock, but it will help everyone on the team get a better understanding of how fast the ice is running that night. This is especially useful when curling on unfamiliar ice. It's also helpful for consistency on takeouts. Many different words are used to discuss takeout weights, but they are either adjectives that have no meaning (firm or control) or distances you should try to throw it (hack, board, through the windshield of my car in the parking lot). I'll be honest, I've been curling for seven years and I have no idea if I've ever thrown a takeout "control" weight. I think some good curler said, "Throw it control weight" to some novices and they pretended to understand what that meant. Those novices then said it to some other novices and now you have generations of curlers pretending to know what control weight is (I did when we discussed what control weight means earlier in the book!). Now, if you tell someone to throw it 14 seconds from hog-to-hog and it times at 12.5 seconds, you have something to work with. It's easier to adjust the speed of your delivery when you have a specific target rather than something vague like "Throw it more control weight," or "down normal," which I've heard used in a game. During the Olympics, skips will discuss numbers in the fourteen range after draws trying to narrow down the speed of the ice.

The third timing method is known as sheet timing. This method starts the clock when the rock reaches the hog line and stops when it comes to rest on the other end—preferably on the tee line in the house. There are adjustments you can make if it falls short or goes long, but let's use our imagination and pretend it lands on the tee. Sheet timing is valuable because it lets you know how fast the ice is running on any given night—at least at the specific moment in time. It's also a method that's delivery neutral since you don't start the stopwatch until after the rock is released and it's very helpful for skips who don't have to throw their last rocks completely blind as to how fast the ice is running.

BASIC STRATEGY

In any given end, it can be hard to tell which team is playing offense and which defense. If you've only watched curling on TV, you might think that the team hitting rocks all over the arena is on the offensive. Stones bouncing all over the sheet, sweepers flying down the ice furiously scrubbing while also trying not to fall over, and violent reverberations of the rocks smashing together sounds like an offensive campaign. However, despite these descriptions, knocking lots of rocks out of play is actually defensive curling. If more rocks are knocked out of play, then fewer rocks can score. Playing defensively keeps the score low and reduces the risk of giving up a big end. In other words, if you come down to the final two stones, and there's only one in the house, the most either team could potentially score is a deuce. On the other hand, guards sound defensive but really aren't. Throwing lots of guards, draws and freezes mean more rocks will be in play and there's a better chance of the team with the hammer scoring multiple points in the end or having several points stolen by the other team.

The fundamental strategy for the team with the hammer is to try and score at least two points. By contrast, the team without the hammer is trying to steal points, or, failing that, force the team with the hammer to only one point. The team without the hammer will typically throw a centerline guard to start the end. The point of this guard is to plug up the middle, eventually making it hard to draw to the button with the hammer or to make the hammer team (Stop! Hammer team!) waste a rock taking that guard out later in the end to get a clear path to the button.

The team with the hammer throws typically throws a corner guard. The corner guard allows them to come around it with a draw later in the end. Depending on where those first few rocks end up will dictate how the end is played. The eventual goal is for the team with the hammer to get a well-protected scoring rock somewhere out on the side of the house in the eight or twelve-foot and keep the rest of the house clean to set up the skip with a draw to the button for a second point. In contrast, the team without the hammer is trying to get a rock in the house and trade hits so that the other skip has no choice but to shoot for a single point.

Of course, this isn't the only way to play an end. In competitive play, the team without the hammer often throws a rock in the house with the idea of making the team with the hammer chase those rocks throughout the end forcing them into a shot where they can score only one point. However, if that rock is behind the tee line early in the end, skips may decide to ignore it completely as there is still a path to the button and an opportunity to get one or multiple points.

Another fundamental strategy can be to blank an end. In a blank end, neither team scores and the team with the hammer retains it for the next end. This can be useful if a team has the hammer in an odd end and wants to flip that to an even end for the advantage of having the last rock in the last end of the game. The skip may also decide that there's a better opportunity to score two points in the next end, so may blank it simply to try again. Blanking an end and retaining the hammer is something you might see later in a game while playing for two points is something you might see earlier as teams are keeping the score low while working to get the feel of the ice.

Shooting Percentage, DOD, and Sweep Percentage

Thankfully, we don't keep statistics during regular league curling. If so, my curling expertise might be severely undercut by some simple mathematics. Most competitive play is measured on a shot-by-shot basis and will either be displayed on the TV, if you are watching the Olympics, or saved in perpetuity on a website like CurlingZone. The three major statistics measured during a curling match are shooting percentage, the degree of difficulty, and sweep percentage. There is other information teams will track. For example, Canadian Gold Medalist Brad Gushue has a teammate track the behavior of every rock during a tournament in a log to use as a guide for picking rocks later in the event or to help with the shot call process for his most important shots. I don't have that compulsion for details, so we'll stick with explaining the three most likely statistics displayed on a television during the Olympics.

Shooting percentage is calculated based on how close the shooter came to hitting the shot the skip called. The result of the shot is irrelevant. If the skip says, "hey buddy, throw the rock a hundred miles an hour and hit the guard on the nose," and the shooter throws it a hundred miles an hour and hits the guard on the nose, the shot is scored a four. It doesn't matter that the guard he or she hit goes back into the house and knocks all the shooter's team's rocks out of play. They hit the shot that was called. Scoring of each shot ranges from 4 (completely accurate) to zero (oops). If a player is called to throw it through the house and they do that successfully, the rock isn't counted as part of their shooting percentage (think of a walk in baseball). On the other hand, if a player hits a particularly difficult shot in a critical part of the game, that shot could be scored as a five depending on the generosity of the scorer. These are the shots on YouTube where you gather the entire family around the computer to watch while your spaghetti boils over in the kitchen.

Judging shooting percentage requires someone with a deep familiarity with the game. Sometimes a skip simply puts the broom down without going through the motion of calling an entire shot, and the scorer will have to determine what the skip wants. Other times multiple similar outcomes are acceptable and should be understood when scoring. With that in mind, scorers tend to err on the side of scoring each shot with a higher number rather than a more severe level of harshness.

Players are not only graded on whether they hit the shot called: Degree of Difficulty (DOD) is also tracked during competitive matches. DOD is a subjective measurement of the scorer. It's measured on a scale of one (throw a guard on an empty sheet) to five (throw a double runback triple for two). DOD gives the viewer more depth to a player's performance than simply shooting percentage would along. If a player is shooting 70% with a 1.25 degree of difficulty, you know they aren't curling as well as a player with a 70% shooting percentage and a DOD over two. It's important to remember these measurements have an element of subjectivity. Player performance statistics like shooting percentage and degree of difficulty straddle the line between something clearly objective, like shooting percentage in basketball, and something more subjective, like scores given to fancy horse dancing at the Summer Olympics.

In addition to scoring the shot for accuracy and degree of difficulty, the sweeping percentage can be calculated for each thrown rock. Calculating sweeping percentage involves the most straightforward method. It's the amount of distance that the rock was swept from the time it is released to the point where it comes to a rest. Swept about halfway down, that's fifty percent. If sweepers were on a full fourteen seconds as it travels down the sheet, the sweeping percentage would likely be above 90%. Add up all the percentages and divide it by the number of shots the player has thrown. If that number is still over 90%, they are likely to have some very disgruntled teammates.

Scoring and the Scoreboard

After each team has thrown their sixteen rocks, the vice-skips survey the house to determine the score. All rocks in the house are potential scoring rocks. To be in the house, the rock needs to just be overtop of some paint. The vice-skips then decide which rock is closest to the center of the house, and that team scores at least one point with this "shot rock." Vice-skips then continue to count the rocks closest to the center and the team with shot rock keeps scoring until a rock of the opposing color is closest. Teams can score from one to eight (called an eight-ender and it's very rare) points in each end, but only one team can score. If there are no rocks in the house after all sixteen have been thrown, that's a blank end.

Televised curling uses a baseball style scoreboard. Because of its familiarity, it's easy to track the score and who has the hammer in the current end. It also means scorers need to have lots of numbers to hang on the scoreboard to manage all the various permutations of scoring. Think about Fenway or Wrigley field and how many different 0's, 1's, and 2's they need to have on hand to make sure they don't run out during a game. To alleviate this problem, curling club scoreboards are a little different. Some genius (and this person should get a Nobel in Economics, Peace, or Chemistry) realized if you paint the score on the board say, one to twelve, and then have a series of hooks above and below those numbers designating the rock color, vice-skips could hang the end under the appropriate accumulated score.

For example, if the red team scores two points in the first end, you would hang the number 1 (identifying the just played end) under the number 2 (identifying the cumulative score) on the board. If the red team scores two more in the second, you would hang the 2 under the 4. That way, you know the score is 4-0 after two ends. While that sounds straightforward when you read it, most people struggle with this style scoreboard for several games until they get the hang of it. Another advantage of this scoring systems is that a quick glance at the scoreboard tells you who has the hammer-- i.e. the team who didn't score last.

Speed of Play and Thinking Time

You might wonder why the first few ends of a competitive curling match blaze along with hit after hit and a few blank ends. One reason for these quick ends is that teams are taking fairly standard shots and trying to get a read on the speed and swinginess of the ice in order to take advantage of this knowledge later in the game. Another reason for speed is that teams are trying to conserve thinking time for later in the game when it really matters. Recreational curlers complete an eight-end game in about two hours or a little more, and elite curlers can complete ten ends in about two and a half hours, including a fifth end break. While those are particularly stringent constraints, teams do run into challenges when it comes to managing time during a curling match.

Time constraints are particularly challenging in club curling when compared to competitive curling. Some teams are slower than others. As new curlers, my team would agonize over shots that we were never going to hit before going to the other end of the ice to miss it. Etiquette suggests you should play quickly, and most clubs do their best to combat slow play every year.

There are numerous steps curlers can take to move the game along and allow both teams to get into a rhythm. Be in the hack and ready to shoot when the previous play finishes. Not repeatedly getting caught behind the sheet when it's time to sweep because you were grabbing a swig of beer. All that time not being ready quickly adds up over the course of multiple ends. New curlers often want to put the rocks away in perfect order after every end. If that takes forty-five seconds each end it consumes nearly five and a half minutes over the course of a game. As I mentioned earlier, my home club replaced the number of the rocks with letters and removed the temptation to put them back in an orderly fashion. Now, the only way to distinguish between rocks is by their color and the sponsor on the handle. "Awww, you saved my rock for me to throw" is something I say pretty regularly. Touching, really. The lesson is that it's much quicker to toss the rocks to the back and pull out the appropriate one when it matters rather than let your OCD tendencies take over and place them in perfect order after each end.

In club play, there's very little you can do to encourage everyone to speed up the game. Instead, most clubs have a buzzer (or giant cowbell that was carried over from Europe on the lap of one of our members) that goes off an hour and thirty-five minutes in the game telling teams to hustle up and finish the end they are playing, and they can only start one more after that. When I first started curling, we were excited to get six ends in, now when I'm playing another experienced team, it's not unusual to be wrapped with a full eight ends before our time is up. However, we don't really have anything other than the buzzer to moderate the amount of time it takes to play an eight-end game besides other than passive-aggressively glancing at our opponents while they wind down the clock to 8 pm and the end of our scheduled draw time.

If you are watching curling on TV, you may notice in the background red and yellow clocks where only one is counting down at any one time. Those two clocks are measuring think time for each team. Competitive curlers have already conquered those slow play problems that plague club curlers. For them, the shot selection is significantly more complex and while teams may hustle through the first few ends, the amount of discussion later in the game can drag on as teams look for the perfect angle and weight to maximize their shots. Since you can't really use a buzzer in competitive curling, think time controls the speed of play. Both teams get thirty-six minutes of think time for an entire ten end game. That's not a lot of time in the grand scheme of things. It's about 28.5 seconds for each rock. The clock starts when the shooting team's skip takes control of the house and stops when the shooter's rock reaches tee line on the side of the sheet they are shooting from. The clock then stops, and the other team's clock begins once the skip starts the process of determining the next shot.

Announcers may make a comparison to previous timing methods where the clock was running until the stone came to a stop. In that instance, teams that were playing more aggressively with more guards and draws were burning time faster than teams who were throwing hits. The team making the game more exciting by putting more rocks in play were being penalized at the end of the game because their rocks took longer to travel down the ice. The current measurement method gives both teams an equal amount of time to call shots and teams aren't rushing to make up for their slower moving rocks.

You might be wondering what happens if a team runs out of time in an Olympic game. The short answer is they lose. The game is forfeited by the team flashing zeros on the clock. This can create additional, unexpected, excitement at the end of a game. In the 2018 US Olympic Trials, Team Birr was leading by one in the tenth end of his game against Team Brown who had the hammer. With two more shots left, Team Brown only had fifty-eight seconds of think time left. His first shot, an angle raise to the button was rushed and he ended up hitting the rock on the nose, missing the shot entirely. He released his second shot with only five seconds of think time left (at this point I was screaming at the TV), hit the angle raise and came up inches from tying the game. Think time can move what is a thoughtful, and sometimes plodding game, into a hurried flurry of activity right at the end.

OTHER TYPES OF CURLING

In curling, mixed describes an equal gender composition of a team and not cocktails as one very surprised team of novice male curlers learned when they arrived at the Rice Lake Mixed Bonspiel last spring. All reports from the spiel said the guys had a good time, even if they were a little embarrassed, and were likely not to make the same mistake again. I really enjoy my Friday night mixed league. We get out on the ice every two weeks to throw some rocks and eat potluck dinner with the other teams. One week it's taco night and the week after it's a good old-fashioned Minnesota potluck with green Jell-O salad. We don't keep standings in our mixed league, so winning isn't necessarily measured by how many points scored, but rather by how many delicious dishes were brought. Unfortunately, mixed curling isn't an Olympic discipline, so we aren't going to spend a lot of time on it in this book. To be fair, a cooking and curling show might not be that exciting. "I can't go out tonight, you guys. I've been watching this episode of *Crockpot Curling* for six hours and I can't leave before the hotdish starts to bubble!" Both wheelchair and mixed doubles are very similar to standard curling, but with some slight tweaks that alter the game. Unlike my Friday night mixed league, both are Olympic disciplines.

Wheelchair Curling

My exposure to wheelchair curling has been limited to sitting in the bar at the Four Seasons Curling Club while waiting for my league to start later in the evening. Since Four Seasons doubles as the Olympic training facility, several times I've been there to catch a peek of wheelchair curlers practicing before a big event, such as national trials. Even with such limited exposure to the sport, I can say that wheelchair curling is as impressive to watch as it is cold to play.

Wheelchair curling is managed by the World Curling Federation and teams are mixed with four players on each team. The game has moved swiftly from a seminar in Switzerland attended by three teams where they discussed potential rules for the sport in 2000, to wheelchair curling being added to the 2006 Torino Paralympic Winter Games. In wheelchair curling, sweeping is prohibited, and that's basically the biggest difference from the traditional game.

Other than the lack of sweeping, delivery is the biggest difference between the disciplines. After positioning their chair near the hog line and on the centerline and locking their wheels, players can either lean over and throw the rock from a sitting position or they can use a delivery stick. Very few wheelchair curlers have arms long enough to be successful leaning over for a hand delivery, so delivery sticks are the preferred method to throw a stone rather than doing hours of daily arm stretching exercises. Delivery sticks are a straight broom handle with a plastic tube on the end that fits over the rock handle. The tube releases when the rock is pushed and twisted by the shooter and sending it down the ice with impressive accuracy. In all instances of delivering a stone in a wheelchair, the shooter's feet cannot touch the ice while their wheels must stay in contact with the ice.

One of our club's most experienced curlers is always reminding newbies to get out on the ice and cool down their slider before a game. I explained to him that for the month our locker room was without heat, I was getting there early just to warm up my pants, and chilling my slider was just an unpleasant side effect. Cooling down is particularly important for wheelchair curlers. Not to cool down their sliders, as they aren't using them, but to cool down their wheels. Since wheelchairs are stationary during the delivery process and between shots, warm wheels can slightly melt the ice. Since players are delivering at the hog line, you don't want small wheel ruts melting into the ice and affecting the path of the stone as it nears the house.

To be eligible for wheelchair curling, the player must not be able to walk more than short distances without the use of a wheelchair. To play, all a curler needs is to generate enough force to send the rock to the other end of the ice from a stationary position in the chair. They also need to be able to tolerate the cold as there's no sweeping to get the blood flowing and keep the body temperature up. Finally, wheelchair curlers need to be able to tell the same lies over a beverage after the game as any other curler—many of which I got to hear in the bar after the wheelchair camp at Four Seasons.

Joel Ingersoll

Mixed Doubles

Mixed doubles is the new and exciting event at the 2018 Winter Olympics. Having been developed less than twenty years ago and not reaching its current form until three years ago, mixed doubles is not only going to be new to the viewers watching on TV, but it relatively new to the curlers themselves. While it's still throwing rocks down the ice and sweeping, it's the modifications to the sport that make the style of game new.

The gameplay in mixed doubles is like regular old curling with a few exceptions. First, there are only two players on a team and each team consists of one man and one woman. Second, each team only throws five rocks in an end, with one player throwing the first and last rocks and the other throwing the three middle ones. To make things more exciting/confusing, these roles can switch from end to end. The sixth rock for each team is placed on the ice. One rock on the centerline in the back of the four-foot and the second rock as a centerline guard. The team who didn't score in the previous end gets to pick which rock they want. You'll note I didn't say the team with the hammer because (hang on this is where it gets really confusing) the team who didn't score would normally have the hammer, but instead they get to pick the rocks. The team who has the guard throws first regardless of who scored in the previous end.

One time per game, each team can call a PowerPlay where the pre-set stones are moved to the side to set up a corner guard scenario. If your head isn't already swimming, mixed doubles also has a modified free guard zone. No rock can be hit out of play, including the set stones and any others in play, prior to the fourth rock thrown. In other words, five rocks are in play between the teams before anything can be taken out.

These complicated rules ensure that mixed doubles games have tons of rocks in play, and players are hustling up and down the ice. With a recent change that eliminated the requirement for someone to hold the broom for each shot, the game zooms by. I watched three concurrent games of mixed doubles live during the 2017 Continental Cup, and the action and intensity were extreme. I was excited despite missing the opportunity to see a bunch of cool shots because I was watching the wrong sheet. Mixed doubles will be twice the fun when we are all able to focus on one game, and how hard the curlers must work to get the most out of these tandem teams.

Mixed doubles debuted at the Continental Cup in 2001 as an additional event to make the Cup even more exciting. It wasn't until 2007 that mixed doubles took the form it has today with only one man and woman on each team—prior to that there were additional sweepers along with the two designated throwers. In 2008, the very first mixed doubles world championship was held. Early on, Switzerland dominated mixed doubles and won five of the first eight world titles.

In 2018, mixed doubles will make its debut at the Winter Olympics and I'll be particularly interested in seeing how audiences enjoy it. I think there will be teams who treat this event as a side project to their regular competitive teams. "Hey, you're a good curler and I'm a good curler. Let's play together." Other teams will be focused as a mixed doubles team. "We have a country of twenty million people and only six of us curl. Let's play together because we have no other option." For example, countries like France, Hungary, and Austria all have had success in international mixed doubles competition even though they don't typically compete at an elite level with traditional men's and women's teams.

Countries that have had success with traditional curling are also treating mixed doubles differently. The United States representatives, siblings Matt and Becca Hamilton, are also representing the United States in the traditional discipline. However, in Canada, players from Team Homan and Team Koe are not allowed to pull double duty at the Olympics.

THE SPIRIT OF CURLING

C urling is the only sport that I'm aware of that has an actual mission statement. Both the USCA rulebook and the World Curling Federation handbook publish the text in full:

Curling is a game of skill and of tradition. A shot well executed is a delight to see and it is also a fine thing to observe the time-honored traditions of curling being applied in the true spirit of the game. Curlers play to win, but never to humble their opponents. A true curler never attempts to distract opponents, nor to prevent them from playing their best, and would prefer to lose rather than to win unfairly. Curlers never knowingly break a rule of the game, nor disrespect any of its traditions. Should they become aware that this has been done inadvertently, they will be the first to divulge the breach. While the main object of the game of curling is to determine the relative skill of the players, the spirit of curling demands good sportsmanship, kindly feeling and honorable conduct. This spirit should influence both the interpretation and the application of the rules of the game and the conduct of all participants on and off the ice.

The Spirit of Curling is taken very seriously by players whether they know it or not. It's not some Yoda-like mystical power to guide the rocks, but rather it's a blueprint on how to play the game the right way. It guides the match from the pre-game introductions and handshakes, all the way through planning potlucks after a game on a random Wednesday in December (at this point in the book, I think it goes without saying that I love food which springs forth from a crockpot). The Spirit of Curling forms the principles that dictate that skips solve conflicts or disagreements on the ice with limited participation from officials, and why the game's rulebook is so short.

A few years ago, we left the friendly, and very chilly, confines of the Frogtown Curling Club for a Five-and-Under bonspiel at a different club. In our first game, not only we were struggling because we were new curlers, we were also challenged by unfamiliar ice. In our first game, we were getting absolutely demolished. After three ends, I looked at the other skip and said, "There's no way we can win this game, so we are going to concede, but can we at least play the rocks back to the home end?" He agreed that would be fine, and with the reduced pressure of not trying to win a hopeless game, we played a practice end. Our team was able to relax and focus on throwing better and led to us winning our next three games and the second event.

On one hand, we weren't going to win that game, so it's considered inappropriate to make the other team continue to play. On the other hand, we clearly needed some practice if we wanted to be successful. This whole process of conceding the game but playing a little longer is just one way etiquette guides players on the ice to play with good sportsmanship and play the game in a way that represents the Spirit of Curling.

Bonspiels

I don't hunt and, after spending a young adulthood working at a marina where I counted earthworms into Styrofoam cups for hours on end, I don't often fish. This means my only opportunity to get out of the house for an entire weekend to drink too much beer, eat too much food, and tell too many tall tales is at a bonspiel. One of the things non-curlers inevitably get wrong is calling every curling match a bonspiel. Tuesday night league isn't a bonspiel, even if you wake up with a beer-induced headache the next morning.

A bonspiel, or bonshhhhpiel, if you prefer a more German, spittle-driven pronunciation, is Canadian for quinceañera. It's a fun word to say, and I might suggest you use it as often as possible, but every game isn't bonspiel. We aren't bonspieling it up on eight sheets each night. The word bonspiel has evolved from referring to a single curling match and now means a weekend curling tournament.

This makes sense as the earliest bonspiels involved communities getting together to curl on frozen lochs, drink booze, and eat brown meats and peas.

Today there are two types of bonspiels: cash spiels, which are generally very competitive in nature with some sort of prize money, and fun spiels which don't get competitive until Sunday morning, maybe, and the real prize is bragging rights. Fun bonspiels typically are advertised as follows: 3 game guarantee, lunch, and dinner included, drink specials, $300 per team. So, for $85 you get to play 3-5 games, eat a couple of meals, and drink either free or heavily discounted beer, so it makes for a pretty good weekend.

Consensus is the word derived from either Dutch or Low German with it being the combination of "bond" meaning "league" and "spiel" meaning "game." Some holdouts argue that it's Gaelic in origin with "bonn" meaning "coin" and "spiel" meaning "skate." This Scottish origin story seems much more motivated by nationalism than scholarship. Most consider bonspiel to be a term specific to curling, but as Oliver Paul Monckton points out in his book, *Pastimes in Times Past*, "It is a mistake to suppose that the word 'bonspiel' was used exclusively in curling. It was used of archery as well, and used in a sense which makes one suppose that the term meant a friendly intercourse, involving trials of skill of all kinds; and as a word is known to be of foreign origin." While friendly intercourse during the match would certainly make archery just that much more interesting, or dangerous, today the word bonspiel no longer refers to a "shooting things with a pointy stick" contest.

Bonspiels are designed with the Spirit of Curling in mind: "While the main objective of the game is to determine the relative skills of the players, the Spirit of Curling demands good sportsmanship, kindly feeling and honorable conduct." The second half of this sentence if what most people focus on when it comes to curling, i.e. not being an on-ice jerk pants. It's the first clause though, "to determine the relative skills of the players," that makes recreational bonspiels so much fun. Olympic curling is dominated by round robin or pool play. Teams play a predetermined set of games against specific teams and then the winners of each group advance to the knockout rounds. Most elite events are formatted this way. When you get to club bonspiels, however, they really are designed to determine the relative skills of the players and teams, and they ensure that at some point you'll be matched up against competition that is similar in skill to your team.

The way that bonspiels manage to sort teams according to their skill is that they provide for a specified minimum number of guaranteed games rather than a more traditional double or triple elimination bracket. If you win that last guaranteed game, only then do you keep playing until you lose. I've curled in bonspiels as small as sixteen teams, three events and a three-game guarantee all the way up to The Big Spiel which has ninety-six teams, ten events, and a four-game guarantee.

A pretty typical bonspiel, and what we will use as our example here, is one with thirty-two teams, four events, and a three-game guarantee. In this typical spiel, teams start in the first event, and if you win your first game, that's where you stay. If you lose the first game, your team drops into the second event. Game two has all the 1-0 teams playing against each other in the first event and all the 0-1 teams playing each other in the second event. Teams in the first event who win stay there with a 2-0 record. If you lose game two in the first event, you move to the third event with a 1-1 record. In the second event, teams that win the second game stay in the second event with a 1-1 record, and teams who lost both of their games drop to the fourth event. Doing this ensures that after those two games, teams should be slotted in the event of their skill level relative to the rest of the teams in the bonspiel. Elimination games then start with game three. If you are 2-0 in the first event and lose game three, you are eliminated. If you are 0-2 and in the fourth event, but you win game three, you are still alive. After game three, half of the teams are hitting the beer and get to sleep in on Sunday. The remaining sixteen teams, four in each event, must get up early on Sunday to curl in the semifinals and finals to determine each event's champion. What this sorting means is that whether you are a brand new to curling or have a team in which the "rookie" joined the rink in 1978, there's always a chance to play for a trophy or plaque.

If the above explanation seems a little abstract, here's an example from one of my recent bonspiels. I was on a team with a pretty skilled curler, his son, and his son's friend (both of whom compete in juniors). In our first game, we played a team who had a combined five years of curling experience among the four players. In game two, we faced a former US Senior Men's National Champion. We hung in there, but were clearly outmatched, and conceded after six ends. In game three, we played a team of similar skill and it came down to the final shot in the eighth end. We managed to pull out a victory, but it was a nail-biter. At that same time, the team we played in the first game was squaring off against another team of new curlers. We were eliminated Sunday morning by a very good team from Duluth, with whom we were pretty evenly matched, but they shot better than we did. On the sheet next to us, the Seniors who beat us faced off with a team anchored by a former Olympian and a head ice maker. All in all, it was a pretty successful weekend. After those first two matches, we curled against teams of similar skill level and really enjoyed the competition. Which, after the beer and pizza, is the real reason we give up an entire weekend to curl when we could be raking leaves, shoveling snow, or comparing car insurance policies and the like.

Broomstacking

A big part of the Spirit of Curling is the friendships you develop with your team and, more importantly, your opponents. One of the confusing things about curling is you often refer to curling with your opponents rather than against them. "Dave? Oh yeah, I know Dave. I curled with him once and he totally kicked my butt." One of the ways you can develop that comradery is through broomstacking. Broomstacking started as the practice of stacking brooms (no, really) next to the fire after a hard afternoon of sweeping rocks on a frozen loch. As you can imagine, a wet broom isn't good for anything except being an insufficient surrogate for a mop. "Angus! My broom is wet again! It's clumping the dust on the floor!" Since technology has progressed to waterproof brush fabrics and we have lockers, there's no longer any need to stack the brooms by the fire. Broomstacking has evolved into a social break during the course of a game. The skips might agree to broomstack after the fourth end, the midpoint in a recreational game, and just mosey off the ice to hang out with each other for a toast before returning to the ice.

THE END (NO, NOT THAT END)

From the earliest curlers sitting down after a game to beef, peas, and whisky, to that weird Wikipedia entry, now removed, about the winners of a match buying hotdogs for the losers, the most important aspect of curling is what happens in the clubhouse after the game is over. Curling is ultimately an excuse to get out of the house and enjoy the company of friends in the middle of a dreary winter. You haven't lived until you've heard an athlete who has reached the pinnacle of their sport tell you they were struggling in the morning game because they had to poop. And that's just what makes curling wonderful. Not pooping per se, but that it's a social game, where what happens at the table afterward is just as important as what happened on the ice.

I was walking into a curling club on a Sunday morning, and I ran into a guy from a team we had played the day before. Nearly every conversation about curling starts with "So, how long have you been curling?"

He said, "I'm sixty-four and I'm still throwing lead."

I explained to him "My wife convinced me to quit playing adult soccer. I was coming home beat up every Sunday, and she pointed out that I can curl until I'm seventy, but it won't be nearly as fun if I blow out my knee."

"She was selling you short?"

"How so?"

"You can curl until you're eighty."

This is not an exaggeration. The mother of a teammate of mine can still throw from the hack and she's in her nineties. She doesn't sweep anymore, but if you've been tossing rocks for sixty or more years, you generally don't have to sweep much anyway. Hearing about her gives me hope that I can still be curling many decades from now. "Just wheel me out of the nursing home and get me to the sheet now, Lydia!"

Curling is booming, at least in the Twin Cities. And during each Olympic cycle, it gets much more popular. When I started curling after the 2010 Vancouver Olympics, the Saint Paul Curling Club was the only dedicated curling facility in town. After finishing a short spring league, we thought we wouldn't get another chance to curl because the Saint Paul club was packed to the gills and there was a waiting list to become a member. The following fall, the Frogtown Curling Club opened, and we became charter members. Two years after that, the Four Seasons Curling Club opened in the north of the cities and was designated the Olympic training facility for curlers. Two years ago, the community-funded Chaska Curling Center opened and nearly everyone in the entire town signed up to curl. In 2017, the Dakota Curling Club went from having games a couple of nights a week on a hockey rink, to having their own dedicated facility. On any given night in Minneapolis-Saint Paul over 500 curlers take to the ice, and that's not including any day leagues or group learn-to-curl rentals.

It's not just the Twin Cities though: From Portland, Maine to Aberdeen, South Dakota, to Orange County, California, clubs are being formed in hockey arenas, and hockey arena clubs are moving to dedicated ice –like in Atlanta. You might not think there's a club near you, but there's a pretty good chance there is and if you're reading this because you were excited by watching curling during the Olympics, there will be an opportunity for you to participate in a learn-to-curl. Pick up some beer and take advantage of it. You'll be glad you did.

GLOSSARY OF CURLING WORDS

4, 8 or 12 Foot: The rings in the house. The numbers four, eight and twelve refer to the outermost distance of the ring from the pin.

Across the Face: A rock that curls from one side of a stationary stone and makes contact with it on the other side.

Angle Raise: Hitting a stationary stone on the outside to move it toward the button.

Arena Ice: A multi-purpose facility where hockey players ruin the ice for curling.

Away End: The end of the sheet to which players aim in the odd-numbered ends (Where you don't leave the rocks after a game if you don't want the ice maker mad at you).

Back 4, 8 or 12: Locations in the house behind the tee line.

Board Weight: A heavy takeout such that the stone travels all the way to the bumper or backboard if you miss the target.

Back End: The skip and the vice-skip.

Back Line: The line behind the rings of the house. A rock must go completely past the back line in order to be out of play.

Back of the House: The semi-circle of the house that's behind the tee line.

Biter: A rock that is partially in the twelve-foot.

Biter Bar: A metal bar that is placed in the pin in order to measure twelve feet from the center of the house. It can only be used to measure if a rock is in the free guard zone or in the house at the beginning of an end or if a rock is in scoring position at the end of an end.

Blank End: An end which neither team has a rock in the house, so no points are scored. You cannot divide by a blank end.

Blanking an End: Intentionally throwing the hammer in such a way as to ensure no one scores in an end. This can be accomplished by intentionally throwing through the house or a hit in which the skip's rock also goes out of play.

Bonspiel: A drinking tournament that also involves curling.

Bottle Skip: The fifth player on a recreational team who isn't curling and oversees making sure their teammates' beverages are always full.

Broom: Where a broom pad is placed on the ice as a target for the shooter. When a player misses that target, it's called being off the broom.

Broomstacking: Two teams taking a mid-game break off the ice for a drink.

Brush: Another word for broom and sweeping.

Buried: A rock that is furtively hiding behind one or more guards that a shooter can't see from the other hack and cannot be directly taken out.

Burn: A player making contact with a moving stone.

Burned Stone: A rock that is taken out of play because a sweeper made contact with it while it was moving.

Button: The smallest circle in the center of the house.

Cash Spiel: A bonspiel that offers a cash prize for the winners.

Center Guard: A rock on or near the centerline and in front of the house. Intentionally thrown by the team without the hammer in an attempt to make it harder to draw to the button.

Centerline: A line that runs from one backline to the other backline and marks the middle of the ice.

Christmas Tree: When a team gets a rock in the house and is then able to place more stones in front of that stone in a triangle shape. Also, not what Charlie Brown brought home for Christmas.

Circles: Another name for the rings or a college radio hit for Soul Coughing in the early nineties. Generally, this book doesn't refer to this song.

Circus Shot: A low percentage shot intended to move a bunch of rocks around in an effort to score.

Clean: Light sweeping in front of the rock to make sure a rock doesn't pick on its path down the ice.

Come Around: A draw that curls behind another rock.

Coming Home: The last end of a game. It's either the eighth end in recreational curling or the tenth in competitive curling.

Concede: To admit defeat and shake hands with your opponent to signal that the game is over and it's time to get a beer.

Control Weight: A lighter takeout where the delivered stone is expected to stay in play.

Corner Guard: A rock thrown short of the house and on either side of the sheet. The team with the hammer will throw these at the beginning of the end in the hopes that they will be able to draw around it later in the end.

Cutter: A rock that curls more drastically than the other rocks it's paired with.

Curler: A person who shot much better after the game than during it.

Curling: The reason you are reading this book.

Delivering End: The end the team is shooting from.

Delivering Team: The team currently throwing a stone.

Delivery: The process of not falling down while pushing from the hack to release a stone.

Delivery Aide: Also known as a stabilizer. A plastic device that can be used in place of a broom while shooting.

Delivery Stick: A broom handle with an attachment that affixes to the curling stone to allow wheelchair curlers or players with injuries to throw without pushing out of the hack.

Deuce: Hitting two rocks out of play or scoring two points in an end.

Displaced Stone: A stationary stone that was struck and moved by a delivered stone.

Double: A shot that hits two stones or a size of delicious alcohol-based beverage.

Down Weight: A hit that is thrown lighter than a normal takeout.

Draw: A shot intended to finish in the house without making contact with another rock.

Draw Weight: A rationale for why a player can't make their draws i.e. "I can't seem to find my draw weight tonight."

Drawmaster: A very important person who puts together the brackets for bonspiels.

Eight Ender: Scoring eight points in a single end.

Electronic Hog Line Device: Another way humans are being replaced by machines. The Eye of Sauron lights up if a player commits a hog line violation.

End: Everyone says it's like an inning in baseball, but there's no guarantee that every player gets to bat in an inning, so it's really not like baseball at all.

Extra End: Like extra innings in baseball (okay that works here). In recreational curling, this might be a four-rock end (each player throws one stone) or just a skip's draw to the button.

Fall: Something that happens with surprising regularity. Also, when a rock moves against its curl.

Fast Ice: A game where the stones travel further than expected after delivering the stone. Also, an excuse for throwing a draw through the house.

Finish: The behavior of the stone during its last few feet of movement. Also, one player sweeping during those last few feet in the hope of getting a little extra curl.

Firm Weight: A heavier takeout typically thrown to move multiple stones.

First Player: The lead on the team. The individual who throws a team's first two rocks of each end and sweeps the rest of them.

Flash: To completely miss everything in the house.

Fourth: The last player to throw in the end. Usually, but not always, this is also the skip.

Free Guard Zone: The free guard zone is all the whitespace outside of the house and in front of the tee line. If a rock is located here, it cannot be knocked out of play until after the fourth rock of the end is thrown.

Freeze: A stone that is thrown to come to rest touching another stone in play. Also, what you do at the Frogtown Curling Club in late January and early February

Front End: The lead and second of a curling team. They get the head part of the horse costume.

Front of the House: The area in the house that is above the tee line.

Frost: A thin layer of frozen condensation on the ice caused by humidity that slows rocks down. As stones are thrown the rock and brooms clear the frost of the ice dramatically speeding up the ice.

Gripper: The most important piece of curling equipment

Guard: A rock thrown short of the house used to protect another rock from being hit.

Hack: Similar to starting blocks for a runner, the hacks are where a shooter pushes from during delivery. Also, this author.

Hack Weight: A takeout thrown with enough force that it would come to rest parallel with the hack if it didn't strike a stationary rock.

Hammer: The last rock thrown in each end.

Handle: The direction of rotation when the rock is released.

Handshake: Signifies the start and end of a game and is a great way to share germs among players.

Heavy: A rock thrown further than it should have been.

Hit: Several types of shots that are thrown to make contact with another stone.

Hit and Roll: Throwing a stone in order to hit a stationary stone and move the shooter to another part of a sheet. For example, a rock that strikes an opponent's stone to knock it out of play, and then roll behind some guards.

Hit and Stick: A hit thrown to strike another rock dead center and stop exactly where it made contact.

Hog: To commit a hog line violation.

Hog Line: The thick line twenty-seven feet from the back line on both ends of the ice.

Hogged Rock: A rock taken out of play after a hog line violation.

Hold the Broom: To call a shot.

Home End: The end of the sheet where the rocks are thrown in the even ends. This is where your beer is usually located and often closer to the bathroom.

House: The giant bullseye on the ice. In outdoor curling, it's also a target for birds during the game.

Hurry Hard: A common term used by the skip to suggest the sweepers stop meandering next to the rock and actually sweep it.

Ice: The slippery and hard playing surface. Also, what the movement of the broom is called when setting up a target. Moving the broom further away from the target gives the shooter more ice while moving it closer to the target gives less ice.

Icemaker: If one is reading this right now, know that I recognize you as the most important person at a curling club.

In-Off: Hitting a rock in the outer rings on the inside with the intent to roll the shooter to a scoring position.

Inside: Missing the broom by throwing closer to the center of the ice than what was called.

In-Turn: A rock that is thrown with clockwise rotation for a right-handed curler.

Jam: When a stationary rock is hit by the shooter but isn't moved out of play because it's stopped by rock behind it.

Keen: Ice that curls more than expected.

Last Stone Draw: A series of draws at a tournament that are thrown during practice. The team whose rocks have lowest cumulative distance from the pin gets the hammer in the game.

Lazy Handle: A rock thrown with little rotation.

Lead: The first person to throw for each team in an end.

Lid: Another name for the button.

Light: A rock thrown with insufficient weight to make it to the called destination.

Line: The sweeping call

Lying: How many potential points a team might have at any point in a given end. Also, how many points a team scores at the end of an end as in, "we're lying two."

Measuring Device: A bar with a gauge on it that can be placed in the pin and spun around the house to determine which rock is closer to the button.

Missed the Broom: When a shooter fails to release the rock on target as in, "you missed the broom by two inches."

Mixed: Teams that are comprised of an equal number of men and women.

Narrow: Releasing a stone inside of the intended target.

Negative Ice: A situation where the stone moves in the opposite direction of its curl.

Never: A command from the skip that means, "Get ready to sweep any second now."

Nipper: A contraption with a metal blade that is pushed over the ice after pebbling to even the highest pebbles out.

No Handle: A stone that is either released without rotation or loses its rotation while traveling down the ice.

Not Bad: Terrible.

Not Terrible: Pretty good.

Normal: Regular takeout weight for a team. This could be anything really.

Nose Hit: Because curlers like to anthropomorphize things, the nose of the curling stone is the center.

Off the Broom: Releasing the stone off of the called target as in, "you were off the broom by two inches."

On the Broom: A good job by the shooter who released the stone at the appropriate target.

Open: Teams comprised of any combination of men and women.

Out of Stones: When a team can no longer tie or win a game even if an end is completed. For example, a team is losing 8-5, they have no rocks in play and only the skip's stones left to throw. Even though they still have two rocks to throw, they are out of stones because there is no scenario where they can win or tie.

Out of Play: Rocks are out of play when they cross the sidelines or completely cross the back line. Rocks are taken out of play when they are burned or when the thrown rock knocks a free guard out of play.

Outside: When a shooter throws a stone wide of the broom.

Out-Turn: A stone that is thrown with counterclockwise rotation by a right-handed player.

Paper Club: An officially recognized curling club that doesn't have a physical location. Either because they don't have ice or because they hold events in multiple different locations.

Papering the Stones: Running sandpaper on the stones to roughen them up so they curl more.

Pebble: Frozen water droplets on the ice that serve as a running surface for the stones.

Peel: A very heavy takeout designed to knock a stationary stone out of play and have the shooter's rock go out as well.

Pick: When a curling stone gets something under it while it's traveling down the ice and the stone behaves unexpectedly by slowing down, changing direction, or cutting hard.

Plan B: A second possible result for a shot that is different than what was initially called.

Port: A narrow space between two stationary rocks that a shooter can throw another stone through.

Pound: To sweep a rock hard from its release.

Promote: To bump a stationary rock closer to the button.

Puddling: Leaving a body part on the ice for an extended period of time melting it (the ice, not the body part).

Raise: To bump a rock back.

Reading the Ice: The attempt by a team to understand how the rocks will behave during the course of a game.

Rings: The colored circles that comprise the house.

Rink: Another name for a team. Used as a suffix such as "the Shuster Rink."

Roaring Game: Curling's nickname derived from the sound of the granite rocks sliding on the ice.

Roll: Where a rock ends up after striking another rock.

Rotation: The spin put on the rock when it is released.

Run Out of Rocks: Not having enough rocks left in the game to win or tie.

Runback: Hitting a guard or rock in the front of the house with enough force to drive a rock behind it out of play.

Running Band: The bottom of the curling stone that touches the ice.

Second: The player on each team who throws the third and fourth rocks of the end.

Second Shot: At any point in the end, the second closest rock to the pin.

Sheet: What the playing surface is called.

Shooter: The person delivering the stone.

Shot Rock: At any point during the end, it's the rock closest to the button that is also is scoring position.

Skip: The person who manages the game and calls the shots.

Slider: The Teflon that players slide on when delivering the stone.

Slow Ice: Ice that requires more force to get the stone to the desired location.

Spiel: Short for bonspiel. A curling tournament.

Split the House: When a team throws a rock to the opposite side of the house from where they already have a stone in play.

Stabilizer: A delivery device that replaces a broom for throwing.

Stationary Stone: Any stone that is in play and is not moving.

Steal: Scoring points by the team without the hammer.

Straight Handle: A stone delivered without rotation.

Straight Ice: Ice that curls less than expected.

Striking Band: The middle of the curling stone. The part that makes contact with other stones and/or your foot when you stop it.

Swingy Ice: Ice that curls more than expected.

Takeout: Throwing a rock with the intent of knocking another stone out of play.

Tap Back: Hitting a rock lightly with the intent of moving it back toward the button.

Tee Line: A line that runs from sideline to sideline in the middle of the house. It makes a + with the centerline.

Thick: Hitting a stationary stone closer to the middle so it doesn't roll as far after it makes contact with the stationary stone.

Thin: Hitting a stationary stone further away from the middle so it rolls further after it makes contact with the stationary stone.

Throw Home: Playing in the even ends and throwing the rocks back toward where the teams started the game and where your beer is sitting.

Tick: To hit a stone on the side with the intent of moving it to the left or right a few inches or feet.

Tight: Missing the broom by being closer to the centerline than what was called.

Top 4, 8 or 12: The rings before the tee line.

Top House: Semi-circle formed by rings before the tee line.

Triple: Making contact with three stones on one shot.

Up Weight: A weight heavier than normal takeout weight. Does not require you to loft the rock into.

Vice-Skip: Usually the third shooter on the team. They sweep the rocks thrown by the lead and second and hold the broom for the skip's shots.

Weight: How hard or fast a rock is delivered.

Wick: To hit a rock on the side with the intent of moving it to the right or left a few inches or feet.

Wide: To miss the broom by throwing outside of the target.

Wrong Handle: Throwing a stone with the opposite rotation from what was called.

ACKNOWLEDGEMENTS

Bare Bones Stones: A Welcome Guide to Curling would not have been possible without the help of the following people.

If not for Michael and Erin Gerba, this book would have never been written. I'm much happier (and poorer) since you brought curling into my life.

Fiona Ruthven, Krista Stroever, Rex Huppke, Bob Hedstrom, and Alayne Peterson all read complete drafts of the book at different stages in the process. Their feedback was invaluable, their time greatly appreciated, and I'm very happy my writing didn't kill them.

Jessica Schultz, Anne Farrar, Clint Andera, Jen Antila, and Robert Engberg each read early portions of the book and helped keep me moving forward.

A special thanks to Sarah Bitterman Riddles because otherwise I'd never hear the end of it.

Bill Jordan designed the cover and Duncan York created the graphics. Without which, I've been told, this book would have been as confusing as hell.

Made in the USA
San Bernardino, CA
26 February 2018